Dancing in
the Darkness

"Otis Moss III shows us how we can attune ourselves to God's spiritual direction. He delivers prophetic and life-affirming experiences to help us achieve justice and salvation."

—Dr. Teresa L. Fry Brown,
associate dean of Academic Affairs,
Bandy Professor of Preaching,
Candler School of Theology, Emory University

"Moss takes the words from our ancient Scriptures and prophetically applies them to our most urgent moral battles and choices in ways that make the Bible come alive again."

—Jim Wallis, inaugural chair and
director of the Center on Faith and Justice,
Georgetown University

"Deeply spiritual and socially radical, Moss's sermons and writings speak to this nation like no one else. This book is a wonderful gift to us all."

—Obery Hendricks, PhD,
author of *Christians Against Christianity:
How Right-Wing Evangelicals Are Destroying
Our Nation and Our Faith*

"Rev. Moss III draws from a deep prophetic well and delivers spiritual nourishment that we all desperately need. Moss shows us how to apply the aspirational ideals of the Gospels to address the raw structural oppression confronting our sisters and brothers."

—Dr. Rami Nashashibi,
MacArthur Fellow and founding executive director
of the Inner-City Muslim Action Network

"By making the timeless plea to embrace joy in the face of danger, Moss situates *Dancing in the Darkness* in the enduring legacy of blue note sermons, Negro spirituals, and religious hymns that subvert oppression and transform struggle into spiritual resistance."

—*Sojourners* magazine

"His carefully developed messages build logically, and his words of inspiration seem fresh and attuned to present realities. . . . Moss' advice to 'dance in the dark' is timely and hints at a brighter tomorrow."

—*Booklist*

"Positive, hopeful, and affirming."

—*Kirkus Reviews*

Dancing in the Darkness

Spiritual Lessons for Thriving in Turbulent Times

Otis Moss III

with Gregory Lichtenberg

Simon & Schuster Paperbacks

New York   London   Toronto   Sydney   New Delhi

Simon & Schuster Paperbacks
An Imprint of Simon & Schuster, Inc.
1230 Avenue of the Americas
New York, NY 10020

First Simon & Schuster trade paperback edition January 2024

SIMON & SCHUSTER PAPERBACKS and colophon are
registered trademarks of Simon & Schuster, Inc.

Simon & Schuster: Celebrating 100 Years of Publishing in 2024

For information about special discounts for bulk purchases,
please contact Simon & Schuster Special Sales
at 1-866-506-1949 or business@simonandschuster.com.

The Simon & Schuster Speakers Bureau can bring authors to your live event.
For more information, or to book an event, contact the
Simon & Schuster Speakers Bureau at 1-866-248-3049 or
visit our website at www.simonspeakers.com.

Interior design by Ruth Lee-Mui

Manufactured in the United States of America

1 3 5 7 9 10 8 6 4 2

Library of Congress Cataloging-in-Publication Data has been applied for.

ISBN 978-1-5011-7769-9
ISBN 978-1-5011-7770-5 (pbk)
ISBN 978-1-5011-7771-2 (ebook)

To my daughter, Makayla,
who taught her father how to Dance in the Dark

Contents

Black Coffee Spirituality

BY MICHAEL ERIC DYSON

I have been a Black Baptist preacher for forty-three years now. As part of our tradition, an old saw governs our oral practice. The first time we repeat something great we have heard, we give full attribution, saying, for example, "As Pastor Otis Moss III says." The second time we repeat it, the authorship becomes a bit foggy and obscure, and thus we say, "As someone says." By the third go-round, the fog has lifted, and authorship has shifted as we claim full ownership and gleefully declare, "As I always say."

I want to tell a story that I am sure you have heard because it has circulated widely, so I will spare you the pretense of having authored it myself. Since I cannot determine who first told this tale, I can genuinely begin my recounting with, "As someone says." One version of the story goes that a young lady was complaining to her mother about her troubles and wondering aloud how she would make it through a spell of misfortune.

Her mother led the young lady to the kitchen and filled three pots with water, placing carrots in the first, eggs in the second, and coffee beans in the third. After bringing each pot to a boil, she removed the contents and placed them in a bowl, explaining to her daughter that while they had been subject to the same adverse condition, each element reacted differently.

The carrots had been strong, hard, and unbending, yet emerged soft and weak. The eggs had been fragile, their liquid interior protected by a thin shell, and yet their insides were hardened by the heat. The consistency of the coffee beans remained the same, but instead of being altered by their surroundings, they changed the water in which they were boiled to produce coffee with a rich aroma.

"Which are you?" The mother asked her daughter to gauge how she would respond in the face of difficulty. It is a question we all must answer.

The answer Otis Moss III gives in the splendid book you hold in your hands is that Black folks have been a coffee bean people who practice a black coffee spirituality. We have throughout our history been thrust into various bodies of hostile water—into the Atlantic during the slave trade, and, in the case of the young martyr Emmett Till, into Mississippi's Tallahatchie River. And, each time, we have transformed waters of hatred and brutality into healing streams of moral and social redemption.

We have insisted that God has been troubling the waters—stirring them up, setting up the conditions of healing—into which Black folks have been unjustly tossed. Black folks have consistently proved to be a coffee bean people who change the character of the cultures we inhabit, transforming a nation built on violence and bigotry into a land flowing with the wild aspiration to make the dream of justice a sturdy truth.

Like the coffee bean, Black folks have added flavor and fragrance to a society often bitterly opposed to Black intelligence and humanity.

Black spiritual striving has pushed America closer to becoming a nation inspired to close the gap between its noble ideals and its too often sorry practices. Black people have spilled blood in the soil of American society, and from that soil has sprung a more vigorous imagination about the possibilities of democracy. In this book, Moss beautifully shares the contents of a robust and reflective black coffee spirituality that can once again save the soul of America with prophetic grief, sober redemption, catalytic forgiveness, baptized rage, edifying emancipation, sublime justice, and majestic hope.

Otis Moss III hails from black coffee spiritual royalty. His father, Otis Moss Jr., developed his oratorical skills by speaking out against injustice alongside Martin Luther King Jr. and became one of the greatest preachers in the history of American Christianity. Otis Moss III is a light coffee–colored splash of Black masculinity—a Hollywood-handsome wordsmith whose sacred rhetoric drips with the imperatives of Black prophetic urgency. His parish is a classic black coffee congregation shaped by the provocative oratory of its previous shepherd, the Rev. Jeremiah Wright.

Moss is a magnificent fusion of radical Black theology and uplifting American moral philosophy. No matter how dark the night becomes, no matter how traumatic the times turn, Moss and the people who have loved and shaped him believe that we must never yield to cynicism or hopelessness. Moss is convinced that we must not be carrots that start tough but end soft, nor eggs that get hardened by terrifying experiences, but rather coffee beans that change the cultures and peoples we encounter.

Dancing in the Darkness is a brilliant and poetic meditation on how Black moral genius can transform America. It is a stirring plea for the nation to become a better version of its democratic self by embracing the principles and practices of black coffee spirituality.

Black coffee boosts energy and is rich in antioxidants that combat cell damage and reduce the risk of many ailments. Black coffee is made from roasted coffee beans that are soaked in water that releases their flavor, color, caffeine, and nutrients. Black coffee is the mixture of water and coffee beans without the addition of any cream. And yet, when black coffee spirituality is served to white America, there is in the mixture a deeply flavorful possibility of national transformation that can stir visions, energize belief, revive hope, heal maladies, and change lives. The nation is fortunate to have this opportunity to drink Moss's delicious and invigorating brew.

Introduction

The first duty of society is justice.

ALEXANDER HAMILTON

See how elastic our stiff prejudices become
when love comes to bend them.

HERMAN MELVILLE, *Moby-Dick*

Confront the dark parts of yourself, and work to banish
them with illumination and forgiveness. Your willingness to
wrestle with your demons will cause your angels to sing.

AUGUST WILSON

You have begun reading this book, but I do not know who you are. I do not know your family background, whether or not you pray, your gender, or how you vote. Is there anything we could agree on, any larger project that we share?

I believe, at least, that we share a feeling, a deep unease about this nation. If *America** were music, its chords would be clashing, its

---

*I would like you to imagine, every time you see the word "America" in this book, that the word is in italics, as it is here, to suggest the multiple and intersecting ideas it contains. America is myth and hope, tragedy and invention, and yet fulfillment of the ideal still rests in the possible if we are courageous enough to confront all aspects of its history and face the fullness of our humanity.

rhythm off. If it were a time, it would be midnight, a political midnight in which, more than any time since the Civil War, we are divided: community against community, neighbor against neighbor, citizen against citizen. Elections come and go, but still we struggle to speak across the divides. Has it ever been harder to get through Thanksgiving dinner without an argument?

In 2016, as that unease grew within me, I published an open letter in *Sojourners* magazine to my son, my brown-skinned teenage son, Elijah. Many readers found my letter controversial. It began:

Dear Elijah,

What shall I tell you?

Shall I tell you that your rights are protected, and racism is a scourge now banished from society?

Shall I tell you that in this country, you are entitled to act and live as any other teenage boy, to dance playfully with minor mischief, and to speak with a quick, immature tongue?

Shall I tell you that your body is safe, your mind valued, your future free?

If I tell you these things, my words will be perjury before God and an assault upon the memory of our ancestors. So today I must share a hard truth with you. The truth, my son, is that you are not safe. You are not valued by certain others because of their persistent melanin phobia. There is nothing wrong with you, but there is something wrong with adults who cling to myths created to maintain power and control. You do not yet have the right to be a frolicking teenager like other children in our community, for your boisterous actions might be misconstrued as a fearful threat by people who refuse to remove the racialized lens from their eyes.

My public letter provoked strong reactions. Among my readers who were not people of color, there seemed to be a feeling that I was, perhaps, a little bit stuck in the past. Were we not beyond this racism stuff now? Had we not seen a Black president in the White House?

Among my evangelical readers, there was a different confusion. Why focus on race when we are all one in Christ? Was love not the essential spiritual truth?

Several people of varied backgrounds urged me: *Can't you offer any more hope?*

Many seemed to feel I was withdrawing from them, focusing narrowly on painful, racially motivated events, and turning away from the larger project they had thought we shared. I was asked and asked again: *Why is such a letter necessary?*

The need for my letter—and its connection to hope—was both simple and complex. Yes, I was writing about my concerns as the Black parent of Black children. With the very same words, however, I was fighting for the soul of a nation struggling to be born. To save either, we must save both. Dr. Martin Luther King Jr. articulated this ideal. He called the movement that he led not a movement to advance Black people but a struggle for the soul of our country. I will do my best to explain.

I say we share unease about America in this political midnight, but as much as we fight over politics, our trouble is not, at its root, political. Sure, some policies rightly ignite our passion. Some leaders serve with integrity for the public good, while others use the political podium for their personal benefit. Yet something even more important is at stake, something we feel but rarely articulate. What we yearn for will never be found by rearranging politicians and policies. That, I believe, is why our feeling of unease cuts deep.

Though we may lack the exact words for it, we hope for more than political victory. I believe we hunger for the bread of love wrapped in the actions of a just society. We yearn to embody the promise of our American experiment in pluralism and democracy. If that is true, we can never be fully satisfied by what we find through political systems or social media networks. What we lack never goes on sale during Black Friday or Cyber Monday. We are searching for no less than a new spiritual foundation on which to transform these yet-to-be-united states.

And it's not as if life was so easy before. No life is easy. Troubles pile up so high that sometimes you cannot see past them. Fear, grief, anger, chaos—these are never complete strangers. Challenges come upon us unexpectedly and unwanted, and we must respond, well or badly. As a pastor, I am blessed to enter the lives of the people in my community. I am given the privilege to see them at their best and sometimes to see them spiral into their worst. There are days when we manage to find the light within despite great challenges. We respond from our best selves, drawing strength from our secret inner altar. We gladly offer a brick upon the foundation of a world we yearn to see built. But too often, instead, we let the darkness in. Our impulsive acts add harm to harm. If we own a moral compass, we must have lost it somewhere.

In these troubled times, then, we face a double challenge. We must meet the demands of our personal lives and yet also respond to this nation's profound political and—let me say it—*spiritual* crisis. If we're going to redeem this country, we must keep fighting for it. Maybe you do not expect to hear this from a pastor, but I will say it anyway: We must fight like hell.

Will we find the spiritual resilience and the spiritual resistance for that fight? Can we keep our eyes on the goals that serve our highest values and find the courage and self-control to achieve them? Honestly, it can feel overwhelming. But there is a shared American tradition for us to draw on, guidance from our elders to shine a light. A tradition that speaks to what many on both sides of this divided nation yearn for deeply, something more than the political class, left or right, has the will or the ability to provide.

This shared tradition has a long and varied lineage, far more diverse than many people know. It goes back to the authors of our Constitution, the "founding fathers" who were inspired by the Iroquois nations' approach to group decision-making. It is a lineage that includes Akhenaten, Arete of Cyrene, Aristotle, Lao Tzu, Saint Augustine, Al-Farabi, Maimonides, Zera Yacob, Anton Wilhelm Amo, Frederick Douglass, Sojourner Truth, Antonio Gramsci, John Dewey, Simone Weil, Ida B. Wells, Albert Camus, Reinhold Niebuhr, Thomas Merton, Fannie Lou Hamer, Malcom X, the Sermon on the Mount, the Hebrew Prophets, and the spiritual wisdom of all the great faith traditions of the world. However, it is revealed especially within the Black Spiritual Tradition. The African American experience is perhaps a hundred years ahead of the rest of this country when it comes to living with and making the most of the blessings of diversity.

I talk the way I talk and preach the way I preach out of that tradition, that shared experience. A true child of the civil rights movement, I was born of parents who met while working with Dr. Martin Luther King Jr. and were blessed to have him officiate at their wedding. I was raised with many of the great preachers and political leaders of our time as guests at our family dinner table.

Today, I am a Black, male, midwestern pastor with southern sensibilities, head of an African American congregation. We proudly proclaim that we are unashamedly Black and unapologetically Christian. We are also proudly ecumenical, embracing many traditions and many peoples. This approach is part of my identity and tradition. I do not talk this way despite where I come from, but because of it. I even checked my DNA: Mine is from Cameroon, in central Africa. Oh, and also from Spain and Portugal.

You can say I serve a Black congregation, and that is true, but authentic Blackness demands you become a citizen of the world, mother of many nations. Through harsh history and creative creolization, our community has become a gumbo of influences. We are African and European, African and Asian, or African and South American. We speak English, Spanish, Arabic, Portuguese, French, Patois, Gullah, Yoruba, Xhosa, and on down the list. We are not Black by the social construction of race but by the beautiful, boundless power of a culture where old languages and ancient traditions find a home in contemporary bodies. We are a Black church, descendants of a people who were stolen, trafficked, and enslaved—and within us is the blood of the enslaver, ancient traders, maritime explorers, monarchs, and warriors. It contains the DNA of later immigrants who came here freely, dreaming of a life without the glass ceilings imposed by feudal lords. We have the whole world in our hands and entire nations and ancient empires running through our veins.

I speak the way I speak because the Black Spiritual Tradition is at the heart of this American democracy, with something to teach the world about living justly in pluralism and sustaining community in the harshest of conditions; about the beauty found in ashes and the transformative power of democratic ideals. And although this tradition draws from many sources and owes a debt to a grand pantheon of leaders and visionaries, it is associated above all with Dr. Martin Luther King Jr.

Dr. King is remembered best in this country, of course, for his civil rights battles, nonviolent protests, and speeches. However, while the civil rights movement provided some of the most urgent and demanding tests of his spiritual vision, that vision was broader even than civil rights. Dr. King offered a unified approach to all of life's tests, political and personal, something we can all carry with us as we walk our paths.

Dr. King saw that we are capable of extraordinary feats, yet we often fall short. What would help any of us to live better? "Life as it should be and life at its best," he taught, "is the life that is complete on all sides." He described three sides. The first is personal: authentic fulfillment of the self. The second side is communal: social engagement and responsibility. And the third side is spiritual: our sacred kinship and connection with all creation. That connection is grounded in the understanding that all of humanity has the imprint of the Divine upon its soul. Dr. King liked to talk about the three sides of a complete life as being like the dimensions of a house: its height, width, and depth. If the architect draws the measurements wrong or the carpenters cut one beam too long and another too short, the entire house becomes unstable. In harsh conditions, it could collapse. But if the sides are in harmony, a well-measured, well-built home can endure storms of all kinds, lasting a lifetime and beyond.

In this book, I address the challenges of these dark times to help us restore to our house a spiritual foundation of courage, strength, self-reflection, creativity, compassion, and faith. These are not conservative values or progressive ones, not Democratic or Republican. They are deeply spiritual values that should unnerve both "sides." The binary, two-party frame of our political system is too small to contain the vast, wondrous nature of these ideals. Through these values, we can learn to face and make spiritual use of our fear, anger, confusion, chaos, and all of the other challenges of our political and spiritual midnight. We can rediscover the superheroes hidden within each of us and work to build the nation for which we yearn. We can find the spiritual resistance and the spiritual resilience that it will take.

Let me be clear: I have written this book to bring news that will afflict all who are comfortable. The bad news: It is midnight. But I have also written this book to bring news that will comfort the afflicted.

The good news: It is midnight! You need to understand that when that clock moves from 11:59 P.M. to 12:00 A.M., the new day has come. A new morning is beginning. And in that new morning, we shall rise anew.

Rev. Samuel "Billy" Kyles, one of the great civil rights leaders, used to preach for us sometimes at Trinity United Church of Christ before he made his transition to eternity. He told a story from the time when gas powered the streetlights. A little boy who was supposed to be in bed watched out the window as a city employee lit the lamps. He ran to his mother and father and said, "Come here, quick!"

"Why are you up?" they asked.

"You have to see this! There's a man outside. He's punching holes in the darkness!"

Reverend Kyles explained, "That's your role: To punch holes in the darkness."

I know that we can punch holes in the darkness, for I know that dawn is coming.

If I may offer an MLK remix: Dawn is coming because Thomas Carlyle is right:

No lie will live forever.

Dawn is coming because William Cullen Bryant is right:

Truth, crushed to earth, shall rise again.

Dawn is coming because the Bible is right:

What you reap is what you sow.

And we shall sing the song of that great bard from California, Kendrick Lamar:

We gon' be alright.

1

Link Love and Justice

Learn to Slay Your Spiritual Dragons

The revolutionary sees his task as liberation not only
of the oppressed but also of the oppressor.

STEVE BIKO

Whenever Dr. Martin Luther King Jr. traveled, legend has it, he carried three books with him: the Bible; the Constitution of the United States; and *Jesus and the Disinherited*, by Howard Thurman. Perhaps that third book is not as familiar to you as the first two. Howard Thurman was a Black American who grew up in Florida during segregation. He became a minister, philosopher, and a mentor to civil rights leaders, one of the great authorities on the teachings of Jesus and on nonviolent resistance to oppression, but all of that nearly did not happen. He almost gave up on his education when he was still a teenager.

Thurman recalls in his memoir that in segregated Florida there were separate schools for Black children and Caucasian children.

Public education for Black children in Daytona ended with the seventh grade. Without an eighth grade, there could be no demand for a

Black high school; and if by chance a demand were made, it could be denied on the ground that no Black children could qualify.

After I completed the seventh grade, our principal, Professor Howard, volunteered to teach me the eighth grade on his own time. At the end of the winter, he informed the public-school superintendent that he had a boy who was ready to take the eighth-grade examination and asked permission to give the test. The superintendent agreed to let me take the test, but only on the condition that he examine me himself. I passed, and a short time later the eighth-grade level was added to the Negro public school.

There were only three public high schools for Black children in the entire state of Florida, but there were several private church-supported schools, the nearest to Daytona Beach being Florida Baptist Academy of Jacksonville. A cousin who lived in Jacksonville told my mother that if I enrolled in the academy, I could live with him and his wife, doing chores around the house in exchange for a room and one meal a day.

When the time came to leave for Jacksonville, I packed a borrowed old trunk with no lock and no handles, roped it securely, said my goodbyes, and left for the railway station. When I bought my ticket, the agent refused to check my trunk on my ticket because the regulations stipulated that the check must be attached to the trunk handle, not to a rope. The trunk would have to be sent express, but I had no money except for a dollar and a few cents left after I bought my ticket. I sat down on the steps of the railway station and cried my heart out.

Presently I opened my eyes and saw before me a large pair of work shoes. My eyes crawled upward until I saw the man's face. He was a Black man, dressed in overalls and a denim cap. As he looked down at me, he rolled a cigarette and lit it. Then he said, "Boy, what in hell are you crying about?" And I told him.

"If you're trying to get out of this damn town to get an education, the least I can do is to help you. Come with me," he said. He took me around to the agent and asked, "How much does it take to send this boy's trunk to Jacksonville?" Then he took out his rawhide money bag and counted the money out. When the agent handed him the receipt, he handed it to me. Then, without a word, he turned and disappeared down the railroad track. I never saw him again.

We will never know who he was, that stranger in the railroad station. He left no record, wrote no books. All he did was pour a story into a boy sitting alone at a railroad station, a story in which an impoverished, discouraged Black child was not a second-class nobody with no business even trying to ride a train, but instead the hope of his ancestors, the answer to their prayers, worth comforting, encouraging, and supporting with practical help.

Thurman made it to Jacksonville and went to high school. Overcoming further challenges, he made it to college. In time, he became a minister, the teacher of another young man by the name of Martin Luther King Jr., who took Thurman's works as the basis of his theology. Toward the end of his life, Howard Thurman wrote his autobiography, which he dedicated "to the stranger in the railroad station in Daytona Beach who restored my broken dream sixty-five years ago." That stranger at the station changed history by putting a new story into a despairing Black boy.

Of course, it was not just any story. That story was one of extraordinary nourishment, significance, and power because it combined two elements usually kept separate. First, it was a story of justice. The legal system of the segregated South at that time was saying to this young man that no one who looked like him should ever attempt to move beyond the bounds Jim Crow had set. The ticket seller at that train station wanted this Black boy to be part of that racist story of restriction and failure. He made use of the boy's obvious poverty and a meaningless technicality in the rules—insisting that tickets for checked luggage had to be attached to trunk handles—to keep him in his place. But the stranger at the station told a different story. "Trying to get out of this damn town and get an education," as the man said, was a worthy ambition, a moral and political act that demanded both understanding and support, an act that could remake that young man's life and, in time, reorder his entire society. In this story, young Howard was not a poor nobody but the bearer of a future for which generations before him had hoped and prayed.

The stranger at the station helped young Howard see himself as the hero in the dream of a better life both for himself and his people. In that, it was a story of justice. But at the same time, it was a story of love. The stranger recognized the boy crying on the station steps as a human being, a creation of the divine, loved by God and worthy of human care. To offer that child his gruff sympathy and his encouraging words, his reassurance, and the financial strength to do what the child could not yet do for himself was to give love like a parent gives a child.

The extraordinary power of that story derives from the way it combines love and the struggle for justice. It would have been loving, but not an act of justice, for the stranger at the station to speak kindly to young Howard, to buy him a meal or walk him home. But the danger of love without justice is that it becomes sentimental, even appeasing, like the sentiment of a battered spouse who returns to the abuser out of "love." Had young Howard and his benefactor shared a meal together, they might have felt better for a day about their lot under Jim Crow, but it would not have prevented future suffering. Love without justice would have taken no lasting action, brought no change.

On the other hand, it would have been the beginning of justice if the stranger at the station had cursed the ticket seller, found a way to inflict on him the same measure of pain young Thurman experienced, and gone to join the political fight against the cruelty of racial segregation. But justice without love can become ruthless. An eye for an eye. That kind of justice risks continuing the cycle of hatred and reprisal that can tear down a community. Justice without love destroys. It was the *combination* of love and justice that set young Howard Thurman, his future student Martin Luther King Jr., and the American civil rights movement on a path toward the light.

Now, a cynic might doubt the truth of this story. Thurman remembers a man at the station, but he wrote his book many decades after he supposedly met that man. You can't Google "Thurman station man" and pull up an image or confirm that such a person resided in Florida in that year or frequented any given train station. Is it possible this story isn't true?

Skepticism of this kind misses the essential message. The great stories of love and justice, including many in this book, are *stories*. Their power does not derive from the journalistic precision of those who pass them along. In Africa, the storyteller, called the *griot*, is an elder whose mission is to wrap sacred mystery into the inadequate words of the human vocabulary. These stories are passed orally, changing as they are told and told again, but the changing words reveal lasting truth. Even the simplest children's stories, obviously make believe, can hold extraordinary power. As the writer G. K. Chesterton said, "Fairy tales are more than true, not because they tell us that dragons exist, but because they tell us that dragons can be beaten."

Maybe it sounds odd for a pastor to be talking about dragons, so let me warn you right now: I am just getting started. I talk about dragons, werewolves, vampires, zombies . . . especially zombies. I watch

The Walking Dead and read the comics. And as a partial comic-book geek—okay, a true comic geek, full-on movie nerd, and theological fan boy—I revel in the power of a good story. I share in the fascination with monsters as metaphors and with heroes as paradigms of the possible, whether in comics or graphic novels, books or movies or television, partly because those stories feed my spiritual hunger. They tell me things I need to know. Dragons can be beaten!

When I talk about monsters, I am not just talking about supernatural fiends. The spiritual demons that we meet on our journeys, the ones that threaten to lure us off the path and deeper into the darkness, can be beaten too. So let me offer a little practical advice. If your trouble is zombies, go for the head. But if your demons are spiritual, learn to link love and justice.

This approach, based on the work of Thurman and Dr. King, has nearly been lost. There are many written works that philosophize about the role of love in the development of a civilized society, and many treatises on justice and injustice. Hardly anyone, however, looks at how to bring these essential elements together. Even in the Christian church in America, including the African American church, this Kingian tradition has been largely set aside, if not forgotten, in favor of a new narrative promising material gain, the so-called prosperity gospel.

Part of the difficulty is this strange four-letter word, *love*. We are unable to combine love and justice because we have forgotten what love means. Like so much in our despiritualized society, we have forgotten love's spiritual foundation. When we say "love," we often mean only emotion, romance, physicality, fleshliness. The Greeks had a word for this kind of love, *eros*, which is where we get the word *erotic*. Other times, we mean a vaguely healing, social coming-together: "We should all love one another, brother!" That meaning of love is related to the Greek prefix *phil-*, as in philosophy (love of wisdom), and Philadelphia, the city of brotherly love. However, the Greeks had a third word for love, *agape*. This is the selfless, spiritual love that is described in 1 Corinthians 13:

> [Love] does not dishonor others, it is not self-seeking, it is not easily angered, it keeps no record of wrongs. Love does not delight in evil but rejoices with the truth. It always protects, always trusts, always hopes, always perseveres.

Agape love is the love that seeks to care for what it loves, whether that is a child, a partner, the land we were given, the community in which we live, or the truths we hold to be self-evident. *Agape* love recognizes that we must become stewards, focused not only on the wrong of the moment but on building a better future.

When you start to look for it, you can see examples of love combined with justice where you might least expect it. In the rules of sports, which must serve the needs of all the players, harm to one player is remedied with a chance to address that harm in a way that restores the whole team. If an opposing player hits you during a basketball game, you have been wronged, and it is called a foul. You may want some justice. You could get your justice by hitting the other player in the face. The rules of basketball, though, say that you do not get to punch the other player. Instead, you get a free shot. You have a chance to do some harm to the other player's team within the game, not outside of it. That keeps the game going, while a punch might have ended the game and started a brawl. The other team is motivated to teach their players to avoid reckless fouls in the future because those penalty shots hurt the entire team. In this way, the rules of basketball provide justice in the moment but also serve the future of the game by motivating all the players to play more responsibly.

If you are fouled in soccer, you are allowed a penalty kick. In hockey, if you foul another player, you are taken out of the game for a set period of time and put in the penalty box. The rest of the team has to struggle without you, so again, not only is justice done for the player who was wronged, but your entire team is motivated to teach a reckless player to repair their style of play.

We have the opportunity to link love and justice in any situation in which a wrong has been done. If a child has broken a rule or gone in a direction a parent does not desire, yelling and grounding will achieve a measure of justice. But if your goal as a family member or a teacher is more than simply measuring out the accepted dose of punishment—that is, if you care whether the child repairs what is broken and returns to a better path—then you need to plan and explain a lesson the child can use. Your justice needs to be linked with love.

You will find a version of *agape* love in all of the world's great spiritual traditions. The Buddhist writer Thich Nhat Hanh explained that love seeks to alleviate suffering. If you love someone, he said, then you cannot want them to suffer. So love must work to understand suffering and then to address the causes of suffering. Buddhist love is love linked with justice.

In the Yoruba tradition, ethics are not rooted in the individual but in the flourishing of the community. True love, then, includes respect, diligence, accountability, truthfulness, devotion, and loyalty. Love cannot be love without justice.

The love ethic was central in the life of Jesus, defining what it means to be one of His followers. Jesus taught that you must preach love not by what you say in the pulpit but by what you do, the actions you take from the moment you get up to the time you rest your head on the pillow. In the Book of Matthew, he chides his followers for failing to understand the complexity and beauty of his mission with a story. He shares the imagery of when the son of mankind comes in glory as a king, and describes the king speaking to his followers, saying, "I was hungry and you gave me nothing to eat. I was thirsty and you gave me nothing to drink. I was a stranger and you did not invite me in. I needed clothes and you did not clothe me. I was sick and in prison and you did not look after me."

His followers object, asking the king to tell them a specific occasion when they failed him in one of these ways.

And the king replies, "Truly I tell you, whatever you did not do for one of the least of these, you did not do for me." He is saying that the love ethic is measured by how we care for those least able to care for themselves, whether because they lack food, drink, clothes, a home, a community, medical care, or freedom. His true followers are those who work to drive out fear, address inequality, and confront the opposite of love, which is indifference and hate.

When Dr. King published a book of his most requested sermons in 1963, he had to choose one sermon to provide the title of the book and speak for all the rest. He chose "Strength to Love," because he believed that love was the most difficult virtue to live. The question each of us must ask about love—deep, spiritual, *agape* love—is whether we have the strength of commitment that is required to link love to justice.

2

Consecrate Your Chaos

Pause to Discover Possibility

> In all chaos there is a cosmos, in all disorder, a secret order.
>
> CARL JUNG

> I have great belief in the fact that whenever there is chaos,
> it creates wonderful thinking. I consider chaos a gift.
>
> SEPTIMA CLARK

It was a Saturday morning at home when our children were small. My wife, Monica, and I were relatively new to Chicago and had recently purchased a house and added a new member to our family, a gloriously goofy Labradoodle puppy named Matteo. I could hear my kids laughing and playing with the dog in the basement. Walking downstairs to join them, the first thing I saw was the dog covered in paint.

Paint.

On the *dog*.

And all around him in the basement, chaos: toys, papers, books scattered everywhere. Then I noticed the walls. There were paint handprints and even paint pawprints all over our basement walls!

This was not a profound crisis, no threat to me, my family, or my community; it was just an everyday test of parenthood. Still, it took me no time at all to launch into daddy outrage: "O Lawd . . . what in the world?!"

For those not familiar with Southern Black church vocabulary, "O Lord" is used as the beginning of a nice quaint litany. "O Lawd" is a straight-up prayer of exasperation: please-show-up-right-now-Jesus-before-I-lose-my-mind! *Who was going to clean this mess?*

Rather than acting contrite, my Elijah and Makayla were excited. They kept calling, "Look, Daddy . . . look, Daddy!" The dog was barking. And oh yes, I looked, but all I could see was the mess in my basement. What was the matter with these children?

"Look, Daddy! Look, look, look!"

When you have kids in your home, you need to find some way to get accustomed to chaos, because you are going to get plenty of it. I had experience as a parent by then; I was not going to fly into a rage. But there was a serious risk that in my annoyance at the mess, in my impulse to get control of the situation and make the kids comply with my need for order, I was going to miss what was right in front of me: a hidden, sacred beauty.

Fortunately, on that morning, I was able to take a breath, one breath, and lift myself a little out of my irritation. For a moment, I saw what they saw. Not just a chaotic, rule-breaking mess on the walls—which it *was*—but also a picture: Makayla, Elijah, Mommy, the dog, and me. The children had painted a mural, a family portrait full of their exuberant love. It was even signed—not just by Elijah and Makayla, but also with the pawprints of Matteo. My heart melted.

There was still a mess for the kids to clean up. Rules had been broken. This was no grave injustice, but part of what we do as parents is provide moral and behavioral order: *These are our family rules.*

There are things you may and may not do, and there are consequences if you overstep. In that sense, it was up to me that morning to stand up for justice. The rules were the rules. Lessons had to be learned. Thanks to love, though, I saw something more. I got the chance to see it—a chance I might have missed without even realizing it was there—because I had paused. And in that pause, I had taken a step back and seen the bigger picture. In this case, it was a literal picture, hand-painted and signed by some of those I loved most, right there on the wall in front of me.

What helps me find beauty in chaos? A true crisis—a threat to yourself or someone you love—can sometimes do wonders to focus the mind. In the moment, if we have spiritual practices in place or we are blessed with inspiration, the noise and confusion may recede for a little while, and we may see again what matters. But as we all know, you don't get that kind of clarity every time your blood pressure rises. In the paint-spattered basement that morning, there was no emergency to make me stop and breathe and focus on what really counted. There was no guiding voice I could hear. It was just another mess.

Chaos overtakes us like a storm. It rushes in too fast, rising like a flood. Not an enemy we can oppose or a problem we can solve, chaos is everywhere and nowhere. In these moments, we tense up, falling out of harmony with ourselves and the people around us, and we imagine we must enforce the rules before the chaos becomes unbearable. That is exactly the moment when we need, instead, to take a loving pause, to temper our legalistic drive for justice. Otherwise, we risk missing the good right there in front of us.

To understand the storm of chaos that can overwhelm a community or an entire country, I think first of how chaos afflicts a single person.

I know that demon well. Even in the best of times, a minister must always keep watch for the warning signs of chaos in a member of the congregation. I might notice a regular participant in the community start to withdraw, not talking like they used to, not showing up in the places you expect them. An easygoing person who suddenly has a short fuse. A teenager who loses their independence and starts following me around the church like a shadow. Or a young person who says, with a quick and quiet tongue, "Hey, Rev., can I ask you a question?" Out of nowhere, for the first time since they were little.

These signs go beyond words. The person may begin to move as if the air around them has thickened with anxiety. Everyday interactions with others become heavy and strained. Once that happens, I am certain: Chaos has made her debut as the unwanted guest of the soul.

Other times, people just grab you:

"Rev., I feel like it's all getting out of control."

"The walls are closing in."

"I really need to talk!"

In our darkest times, when the storm sweeps over an entire community, such feelings are everywhere. People who have children or elders worry they can't keep them safe. Those blessed with jobs worry about losing them. Even following the news can be too much to take. People with mental health issues feel even more intensely challenged. People who self-medicate do it more and more. Activists who work in their communities start saying to themselves, "The more I do to fight back, the more the pressure builds. The dam is cracking, and every time I plug a hole with my finger, ten more holes show up." The question haunts us: *When will this end?*

When chaos is general, we may feel we're going in the wrong direction. Is there any way out? We may even wonder if we're cursed.

Struggling in all that confusion, uncertainty, and violence, we become spiritually worn down. It's too hard to keep believing.

We get *tired*.

We think:

My road is too hard.

The powerful will never treat people right.

I've tried everything, there's nothing to be done.

It's no use.

Chaos breeds cynicism and despair. It pushes us toward withdrawal, inaction. For this reason, those who perpetrate injustice often choose chaos as their weapon. When we see nonviolent political protesters charged by police on horseback or counterprotesters in moving vehicles, when a peaceful gathering is confronted with weapons of war, when citizens are beaten with batons or attacked by dogs, we know that the powers that be have lost the moral argument. Their only remaining tactic for advancing their agenda of injustice is to enforce silence. They conjure the demon chaos, trying to use its power to provoke the other side to despair and give up their struggle.

This is chaos as an intentional political and spiritual strategy. We might lament that "the system is broken," but that is incorrect. In this case, the system is not broken. The system works by breaking people. This is the insight that the Black Lives Matter movement helped a wide range of Americans to grasp, from its creation in 2013 to its astonishing growth in 2022. Systemic racism, in the forms of unnecessarily violent policing and mass incarceration, among others, are designed to kill the Trayvon Martins, the George Floyds, the Breonna Taylors. Violent, unpredictable, unjust actions keep the chaos flowing. These actions ensure that African Americans know that however responsibly we drive our cars, we are going to get stopped. However thoroughly we teach our young people to obey the law, our children will get arrested. However many precautions we take to live safely, we will still get shot. It makes no sense; it is unpredictable, unfair, brutal.

That is life under chaos.

The vigilance and anger of these chaotic provocations are exhausting. They are a current pulling us toward despair. At the same time, this state-sponsored chaos serves to reassure another group of people that "law and order" is being maintained. Excessive police tactics are part of a myth that Black and brown people are a danger, and only aggressive policing and extensive incarceration can protect white people. The chaotic lives imposed on one group make another group feel a need to intensify and perpetuate the system. That system comforts one small stratum of people while it disrupts the lives of another and allows the rest to ignore it all, if they prefer.

At least that was how the system worked until the Black Lives Matter movement. The movement did more than call out injustice. It found a way to fight, using the forces of chaos as an engine for something better, turning what men meant as evil to what God meant as good.

To understand how Black Lives Matter harnessed chaos and made it a national force for liberation, it helps to know a little about the science of chaos. In physics class we may have learned the second law of thermodynamics: that, over time, the total entropy of a system can only increase. In other words, systems tend to move from order to chaos. Let me break that down. Imagine you take a video of yourself enjoying an iced drink while sitting in front of a fire. Over time, the ice will melt and the fire will burn out. You can never build a fire that will un-burn or make ice that will un-melt at room temperature; those physical processes go only one way, leaving you in the end, every time, with a lukewarm, watery drink and a pile of ashes: chaos. And you cannot undo it: The only way to see a fire un-burn is to watch your video backward. So how do we fight chaos?

Because it operates under consistent laws, systems that appear to be completely random in fact contain reliable patterns, patterns we can use. Picture yourself on a raft in the middle of the ocean, trying to reach land. The wind is blowing this way and that, and it may blow your raft along with it, but chances are very low that it will blow you where you want to be. There is also an ocean current moving through the water, but it won't necessarily carry you home either. Energy surrounds you, the chaotic motion of the sea, but because you cannot make use of it, you could die out there. The wind and the current are about as useful to you as a pile of ashes.

Now imagine that a sailboat appears. You signal for it to take you aboard. That sailboat is subject to the same chaotic forces of wind and current as your raft, but it makes different use of them. The sails work as what are called airfoils, to harness the airflow and generate force, movement. The boat's keel and rudder do the same thing with the flow of water below the boat, acting underwater like a second set of sails to harness the current. Now, by using those two forces together and combining them in different ways, the boat can be moved—not just in the direction the wind is blowing or the current is flowing, but the direction the sailor chooses. It's even possible to move in the direction the wind is coming from, not by heading straight into the wind (no sailboat can do that) but by tacking back and forth, zigzagging across the wind to get where you need to go. As you sail home, the wind and the water are still as chaotic as ever, but you are making use of the patterns and laws underlying chaos to get where you need to go.

Black Lives Matter was like a new kind of sailboat that harnessed forces of chaos in a new way. The ongoing history of police brutality and mass incarceration is a current that has long run strong in this country, swamping many small boats, drowning untold numbers.

Antebellum, white-supremacist rhetoric is a familiar and destructive wind, and during the Trump administration it was blowing especially strong. But these protesters used the cell phone as a kind of sail, capturing chaotic brutality on video and using its energy to drive people into the streets. The hashtag #BlackLivesMatter turned social media into a kind of rudder, directing the national conversation toward racial justice. Protests led to more examples of brutality captured on video, which led to more protests, until people around the world were protesting—98 percent of the global protests without violence—in one of the largest social movements in history. Black Lives Matter had used an evil wind blowing the wrong way to get the world headed in a new direction.

In the storm of chaos, lost in confusion and disorder, the question we must ask is not whether we are cursed. It's not whether the time has come to give up. The question is whether there might be some way to use the harsh, unpredictable winds and the relentless currents of our lives to get us moving to where we actually want to go. Do we have the spiritual audacity and the practical means to turn chaotic energy to our own purposes?*

When you take on the confusion and the violence and you refine them, purify them into something new, you are doing what in the vocabulary of faith we call *consecrating* your chaos. To *consecrate* is to make holy, to put it into service for good. In consecrating chaos, you engage it, tame it, name it, take what seemed out of control and charge it with a duty.

The model here is the creation itself. We read in Genesis that in

---

*Spiritual audacity refers to drawing on inner resources such as courage, faith, self-love, prayer, meditation, or compassion in the belief that we are designed with purpose and agency to shift small elements in our control that may result in larger changes.

the beginning, "The earth was formless and void, and darkness was over the surface of the deep." Scripture begins with a whole world of chaos. Then God begins to find the possibilities of design in that formless void, separating light from darkness, water from land, and giving them names. God consecrates the chaos, giving it form. It is presented to us as an act of creativity and of choice. God works in the chaotic void until there is order and light, and it is good. The Genesis story reminds us that the void is not as empty as we think. Chaos is never as chaotic as we fear.

How can we find that hidden order to consecrate the chaos of our present day? What do we need? To start, we need a boat. I said that for Black Lives Matter, some key parts of that boat were the cell phones that captured acts of police brutality on video and the social media that allowed people to share those videos and coordinate actions in response. Patrisse Cullors, Alicia Garza, and Opal Tometi, the women who created the Black Lives Matter network in 2013, recognized that they could take a hashtag, a website, and a willingness to take to the streets, and they could build something seaworthy.

To sail successfully, though, takes more than a boat. If you have a boat but no knowledge of its workings and no experience out on the water, you will get in trouble fast. The women who first deployed the hashtag #BlackLivesMatter had not just social media savvy but experience in a tradition of nonviolent protest that had been worked out over decades.

And even if you have a boat and you know how to sail it, you need something more. You need a destination and the course to take you there. That means you have a landmark to sail toward, or if you're on the open ocean at night, then you might use radar or GPS; or, like sailors in the old days, you could get your position and set your course using the stars. The goal of the Black Lives Matter organizers was to call people to action "in response to state-sanctioned violence and anti-Black racism." They plotted their course according to thirteen guiding principles explained on their website. All these principles were expressions of inclusiveness, nonviolence, and restorative justice. They stated, "We intentionally build and nurture a beloved community that is bonded together through a beautiful struggle."

If you do not know your history, that could sound kind of strange. *Beloved? Community?* But students of history will recognize that the goal and the methods of building "the beloved community" were popularized and shaped in the civic consciousness by Dr. King. In 1957, as he set out to gather fighters against the systemic chaos of segregation and poverty in the South, Dr. King created the Southern Christian Leadership Conference. In its mission statement, his new organization committed itself to creating "the beloved community in America where brotherhood is a reality." The civil rights movement *was* the model for an inclusive community in which all had worth and dignity. The movement itself was the experiment that set out to show how it was done. Freedom was the destination, and the creation of the beloved community was how to get there.

A decade later, in the chaos of the late 1960s, as the Vietnam War raged and rioting spread in cities across America, Dr. King chose as the title for his fourth and final book before his murder, *Where Do We Go from Here: Chaos or Community?* For Dr. King, this was the essential choice for America. The beloved community was the antidote to chaos, whether that chaos came in the form of explicit segregation, poverty, or militarism. It was a society of love and just action, where different is not deficient, where we can disagree but still understand that we live under the same canopy as a nation.

Most important, the beloved community was not a place anyone had ever reached. The America that Dr. King was sailing toward was an aspirational vision that America has never lived, a vision of magnificent faith that at the same time confronted the country's deeply troubled history. Only we can bring this vision into being. It is a goal beyond the power of our eyes to see, a star above the spiritual horizon. The leaders of the freedom movement, like the leaders of Black Lives Matter who followed them, were navigating by the stars.

I believe the successes of the freedom movement and of Black Lives Matter grew from a common commitment to spiritual navigation. If we are to learn to consecrate chaos, we too need spiritual navigation. How do we learn to do it? What does it take?

The path to consecrate chaos is not something we must go out and seek. It is one of the gifts we received at birth, though we may not have recognized its value. I want to give three examples of ordinary situations in which people consecrate chaos, to show that even in these diverse moments, there is an underlying unity. I could pick almost any location in which to find these examples, but today I choose a pickup basketball game, a walk downtown, and a visit to a museum.

You are playing basketball. You intercept a pass and take off down the court. The game is moving very fast, it is exciting, maybe nerve-racking. You want to score; you do not want to blow it—what should you do? You could pass left, pass right. You could drive to the basket yourself. Every player on the court is in motion. It is chaos! How do you find the good choice?

Now another example. You are downtown looking to get something to eat when a stranger speaks to you in a way that offends. You answer quickly. He responds just as fast. You do not know exactly why he said what he said, and he does not know why you said what you said, but now both of you are insulted. A situation of emotional chaos teeters on the edge of no return. What should you do?

Third example. You are hurrying through a museum gallery to

catch up with someone when you turn a corner and see a big canvas loaded with brushstrokes but no clear outlines or shape. It doesn't look like something anybody wants on their wall, just a chaos of colors. Maybe you rush on by, shaking your head at modern art. Or maybe you stop, step back, and pause. You have to pause and look again, with a little faith that there might be something worth seeing on that canvas, and then in Monet's chaos of colors you might discover the impression of a garden. It is the pause that gives us a chance to consider what could be and not just what we have known. Is this just a mess, or might it be a Monet?

The experience is similar for the ball player on the court, looking up and down, not sure what to do. There is no one "correct" response. In basketball you cannot keep to a prearranged plan through the unfolding unpredictability of play. But in the chaos of a fast-moving game, it may be possible to resist that temptation to rush a shot and, instead, pause for an instant and spot the unexpected chance to throw a graceful little pass to a teammate who is open.

And it is not so different beefing on the street. Should you escalate? Should you try to walk away? Forces are in motion, too strong to avoid, too urgent to analyze, but the best choice often becomes visible in a moment of quiet. You take a deep breath. You see things another way. You make a little joke that defuses the tension. The best answer often becomes visible to us at a moment of quiet. You have to pause to see beauty that reveals possibility, and it won't be wearing a nametag marked SOLUTION. But it will look surprising and good. Where there seemed to be only disorder, mess, uselessness, you see a way to make things a little more as you hoped they could be, not just the chaos they were.

At those moments, you are not simply receiving a gift. When you see the design in the confusion, hear the music in the noise, look at the blur of moving bodies on the basketball court and see the opening for your move to the basket, the event is not passive. You are the one choosing to slow the pace of your own perception and give yourself over to the confusion long enough to be taught by it. You cannot simply take control of a chaotic moment, no more than you can control the other players on the basketball court, but you can be taught by their movements to see an opening, to connect seemingly random elements into a pattern, to see *what could be.* The confusion must show its hidden logic, the mess reveal its beauty and meaning. Why must it? Because you insist. You choose to pause until you can see a better way.

Two influences on Dr. King, Howard Thurman and Thomas Merton, both spoke of the quiet of the inner life as an altar where we connect with both ourselves and the divine. Thurman observed that people often talk about something we call "uncomfortable silences," but why, he asked, should we be uncomfortable in silence? After all, we are born in darkness and silence, and we spend part of each night silently asleep. This world thinks silence is a problem, that it's too quiet, not productive, that we need some noise; but Thurman saw it the other way.

Sometimes, at the beginning of a talk, Thurman would wait thirty seconds before he said anything at all. Other times, he would wait seven or eight minutes. When you are not used to silence, eight minutes is a long, long time. He believed that until he reached a place of comfort, it was better to rest in silence. Scripture talks about God speaking not loudly but in a still, small voice, suggesting that the way to hear God is to be exceptionally quiet. So Thurman would wait. When I listened to my father's collection of Thurman sermons and meditations, I would wait with him, silently wondering if he was ever going to talk. In time, the spirit would move him to speak.

The silence that consecrates chaos is what prayer is for. As children, we may have learned to use prayer to praise God for His gifts: "God is great, God is good, we thank the Lord for our food." In the popular imagination, prayer might seem like a way of texting a higher-up to send us stuff we need. But Thurman's silence, one in which he waits for the spirit to move him, is another form of prayer, a method of spiritual navigation that we may not find until adulthood, when the responsibility falls on us to be the consecrators.

3

Redirect Your Rage

Harness Your Power

It may be America will be saved by those
America attempted to destroy.
DR. GARDNER C. TAYLOR

Hear this, you leaders of the people.
Listen, all who live in the land.
In all your history,
has anything like this happened before?
Tell your children about it in the years to come,
and let your children tell their children.
Pass the story down from generation to generation.
JOEL 1:2–3 (NLT)

To be a negro in this country and to be relatively
conscious is to be in a rage almost all the time.
JAMES BALDWIN

When I heard about the death of Joseph Graves, a college student in
my community, I felt the old conflict rising again. Joseph had grown

up in our Trinity "village" from the age of two. Jojo, as he was called, helped his momma, Latanda, sell tapes of music and video performances as part of our media ministry. When I asked her to describe him for this book, she said, "Big heart, loved kids, loved to dance."

Home from college for Christmas break, Joseph had borrowed his momma's car and picked up some friends to go shopping. In one store, his friends got into a dispute with some other young men. The friends got scared and told Joseph they all had to leave, quickly, and the three teenagers climbed into the car. Then someone behind them fired a gun. A bullet shattered the rear window and struck Joseph in the back of the head, killing him.

As news of Joseph's death spread, the adults in the Trinity community recognized the need to minister not only to Joseph's family, who were suffering through one of the most terrible losses any family can know, but also to the wider village, especially the young people who had been his friends. Those young people now felt overwhelmed with shock, heartbreak, and outrage. I was afraid that in their pain and anger—in their need to show strength, assert their manhood, and conquer their fears—they would head out to the streets and unleash their impulses in further violence. They might attack the individual who had killed their friend. Or, when they could not identify the shooter, let alone find him, that they would turn their impulsive rage against some innocent.

Conflict flares so fast. A harsh tone of voice, a look that feels wrong, a disrespectful word—and in a flash of anger, we turn against each other. In Shakespeare, when Romeo confronts Juliet's cousin in the street, his love for her gets shoved aside by rage, "and to it they go like lightning," Shakespeare writes. In a flash of impulsive rage, two young people are lost.

When rage flares, it can feel like the most natural thing in the world. I was afraid that Joseph's friends would find a new victim, and then that victim's family and friends would begin to rage against the pain and the injustice of their own fresh loss. Probably they too would imagine that a counterstrike could make it all come out even, but violence works a strange type of math. It refuses to rest on the number one. In our anger, we feel we must settle the score, but scores like that will not settle. Violence demands its own multiplication. In fact, as my wife, Monica, told me at the time, the tragedy was not only that we had lost Joseph, but that we knew already that if the police found the young person who pulled the trigger—if justice was done—then another young man's life would be over. A second family would have to drink from the bitter fountain of grief.

I think about my own experience growing up. As a young kid, I got into a disagreement with my best friend, Nick. He had taken my ball and I was angry. So I jumped him. I fought him until I got my ball back. I brought that ball home feeling proud, but when my mother heard about the fight, she was not impressed. She said, "Never allow someone to have that much power over your spirit." She explained that once someone learns how to get under your skin, how to provoke you into unleashing violence, then you have given away the real power, which is the power of choice. You may feel strong at the moment you lash out, but the truth is, you were coerced. Your choice was taken away from you.

Did my mother's lesson change my young mind? No, actually. I was a boy surrounded by a culture of masculinity that pushed us every day to prove ourselves with shows of strength and violence. My mother's disagreement with that culture, though, did put a question into my head. It started me noticing that there were different ways to direct my rage. I began to pay attention to other models that offered a more spiritual view of strength—for example, in my comic books.

Many of the superheroes I grew up with, who now appear in television shows and movies, are defined by the ways they restrain their powers (or in their case, their superpowers). Any of the familiar superheroes could live, if they chose, as demigods among humans, taking what they want and forcing others to do their will. Instead, they live according to a code that restrains what they can and cannot do.

Batman has access to every imaginable technology, yet he is utterly anti-gun. He will not kill. He even refuses to kill the Joker, the figure who has caused the greatest pain both to him personally and to all of Gotham. Batman believes that guns are an abuse of power. He refuses to live by the values of his enemies, so he keeps to his code as he works for his community. This is true in both his identities, as Batman and as billionaire Bruce Wayne, a philanthropist who carries on his family's tradition of commitment to a decaying city.

English professor Ramzi Fawaz, in *The New Mutants: Superheroes and the Radical Imagination of American Comics*, points out that many classic superheroes were written as social outcasts, often described as physical mutants, who fight for outsiders. As outcasts, they became heroes to America's racial and sexual minorities. These mutants live by a code that restrains their power but helps to uplift communities of outsiders. These are groups that Howard Thurman, spiritual mentor of Dr. King, would have numbered among the "dispossessed," those in greatest need of recognition of their humanity.

The most compelling superheroes, for me personally, include Wolverine and Storm, Luke Cage and Misty Knight, Daredevil, Monica Rambeau, and Black Panther, the Dora Milaje, and Shuri. They all discover that restraining their impulses is a lifelong and hard-won struggle. Through this struggle they harness their power to work for and uplift their community. They become part of a broader shared story, driven by a profound urge to leave a mark for good. There are many names for this around the world. One community names it a blessing while others call it "good trouble," altruism, or *tikkun olam.* These are all versions of the "good" Samaritan story, which is another term for *ubuntu,* an African word that means "I am because we are." It expresses the connection all humanity shares by seeking the common good. Stories of power restrained in the service of a higher calling keep popping up everywhere.

In this way, all these superhero stories echo the story of Christ, whose time on Earth was a three-year ministry of choosing to live as human even though he was God. As a matter of pure supernatural strength, Jesus always had the power to wipe out the armies of the Roman empire that were oppressing his people. At any moment on the cross, he had the power to climb down or even to fly away. The beauty of the narrative is His choice to restrain His power and say instead: *I will bleed, I will cry, I will hurt, and I will die.* Jesus restrained himself so extremely in order that God's love would cease to seem some mysterious force, difficult for humans to understand. Instead, He presented the divine example through a human life in human terms, choosing for Himself a simple—some would say impoverished—existence among people marginalized and despised. And within this life that Jesus chose on the margins, He spent his time with the marginalized of the marginalized: husbandless women, orphans, lepers, the blind, the lame, the colonized, and religious outcasts.

Jesus restrained his power, not to show weakness or accept humiliation, but because it was the only way to achieve the greater good. And this has been true of all of our heroic leaders, Gandhi, Dr. King, Mandela, and many more. To be a real hero, a real leader, you have to know when to hold back and how to redirect your anger. Nelson Mandela walked out of the prison at Robben Island with greater dignity than the one who imprisoned him, then chose to include his great foe in his administration. Abraham Lincoln defeated his rivals for the presidency, then appointed them to his cabinet. Dr. King paid school tuition for the radical student Stokely Carmichael, who had called him a coward but later became a profound and articulate voice for the Black Power movement.

I learned from all of these examples that while there is frustration in restraining your impulses, tolerating that frustration is our one chance to redirect our power to achieve our greatest goals. As Dr. King preached, "Men must see that force begets force, hate begets hate, toughness begets toughness. And it is all a descending spiral, ultimately ending in destruction for all and everybody. Somebody must have sense enough and morality enough to cut off the chain of hate and the chain of evil in the universe." That chain is truly evil. Our impulsive anger may feel justified, even righteous, for a while. But then those unconsidered impulses ravage our world like demons.

Joseph was killed on a Friday night. Immediately, the church began to organize our team of ministers, deacons, youth mentors, and camp counselors, as well as internal and external security. We put out a call to all crisis-intervention workers—counselors, psychologists, and psychiatrists—and any member of the village willing to help redirect our young people, now crying out for justice, away from physical force as their means. We needed help to remind our youth that it would not honor Joseph to do another person harm, that it was in fact far more honorable to march for justice, to help ensure that Joseph's younger brother could go on, and make sure his mother did not weep alone.

We were trying to lift up a more spiritual model of the warrior. Not the Hollywood action-figure version, who gets angry, pulls out his gun, and takes fast retribution that seems simple, clean, and satisfying. *Bang, you're dead. Problem solved.* We needed to give our youth a map and say, Here, look, this is the person you will harm today, but all these people surrounding him will be affected by the damage you do, just as Joseph's death wounded his family, his friends, and so many of us.

To support our young people in choosing spiritual warfare, we organized peace circles, a practice borrowed from Native American and West African traditions. A peace circle is a safe space to express rage without judgment or fear of retribution. Out of the peace circles came the idea to raise money for a reward for information leading to an arrest. Some of our young people launched a Kickstarter campaign to gather donations. They helped spread the word across the Internet. This gave anyone in the community who felt the need to act a chance to do something constructive. The campaign raised twelve thousand dollars in a few days, mostly from youth, as a reward for information leading to Joseph's killer.

We also contacted our local district police, with whom we already had a very good relationship. Officers are invited regularly to the church to participate in community meetings. We make a practice of introducing officers to our neighborhood, our local organizations, and our young people. In the aftermath of Joseph's murder, members of our congregation who were police officers asked for permission from their commanders to be stationed as escorts for our youth when church let out. The police commander came to the church to offer his condolences personally. These gestures of recognition and respect made a big impression on Joseph's friends.

After services, instead of a traditional benediction, we led our young people to the atrium of the church and gave them instructions to march three by three to the street where the killing occurred. Every young person was given two sets of flyers to hand out as we marched.

One flyer asked those in the community to break the culture of silence. It described the reward for information useful to the investigation. The second read: "We're safe, we're here, we're praying." As they marched, our young people spoke to neighbors along the way, asking them to contact the detectives if they had useful information.

After the service and the march on Sunday, many of Joseph's peers still wanted to do more. Talking on Instagram and texting among themselves, they decided to organize a prayer vigil. This was to be a public event held outside of the church at night, planned without the church leadership. When I heard about it, I was concerned. A public vigil was no secure church gathering. Anyone could show up. There would probably be some who claimed to know the identity of the shooter and others who felt loyal to whoever they believed the shooter had intended to hit. When those two groups of young people came together, full of suspicion and pain, I was afraid that the ideal of nonviolence we were lifting up might start to sound like weak and cowardly excuses, the very opposite of justice.

And yet, while I disagreed with that judgment, I also sympathized. I had held that view myself. Although I was raised by parents who celebrated and participated in nonviolent actions inspired by and sometimes led by Dr. King, as a teenager I had little patience for it. I was a full-on fan of Malcolm X—and I use the word *fan* on purpose. Fans come and go. Fandom is not a lasting, thoughtful relationship, not a true meeting of the minds. It can grow into something more serious, but often it just burns away.

As a fan, I was drawn to X's style as a speaker and inspired by his rejection of the last name passed on to him by a slave-owner ancestor. He made me think for the first time about my own name: Otis *Moss*. How did I get this name, Moss? It did not come from Africa. Of course, I had known that intellectually, but Malcolm X helped me voice my sense of outrage at the history we were forced to endure. I was drawn to his early vision of America as a nightmare, a vision that grew in the years that he was influenced by Elijah Muhammad and the narrow nationalism of the Nation of Islam. Malcolm X seemed to be an antidote to the weakness and humiliation suffered under white supremacy, and from that perspective, nonviolence looked like cowardice. I felt a strong wish to be a warrior and protector for my people, as Malcolm X said, "by any means necessary." I wanted to fight back.

I brought that fanboy enthusiasm with me all the way to graduate school, where I took a course with Vincent Harding, a professor of religion and social transformation at the Iliff School of Theology. He had worked with Dr. King and later served as a consultant to the documentary *Eyes on the Prize*. One day in his class, I began to speak out for the right of African Americans to defend themselves, including the use of violence. I got up on my radical revolutionary soapbox and Professor Harding let me go on and on.

Then he played the class a video clip of the Memphis March, the final action with which Dr. King was involved before his assassination. It was a protest in support of sanitation workers—"garbage men"—in Memphis who were demanding fair wages and carrying signs that read I AM A MAN. With this action, Dr. King was broadening the scope of the Freedom movement, expanding it to acknowledge not just racial but economic injustice in what was called the Poor People's Campaign.

After Professor Harding showed the clip, he asked the class, "What did you see?"

"We saw people marching."

"No," he said.

He showed the clip again.

As we watched more carefully, we began to notice *who* was march-ing. The protesters included some small children, a person with one leg, elderly people. He said, "Otis, when you take the perspective of using violence as a tactic, then the movement ceases to be democratic. Because, in your revolution, the differently abled cannot participate. Children cannot participate. The elderly cannot participate. You are glorifying healthy men, putting everyone else on the sidelines."

It was a philosophical idea, but it hit me in the gut. My fan's ro-manticism about self-defense had been revealed as a fantasy of strong men taking charge and leaving the rest to wait for rescue. It was a patriarchal, misogynist dream. For the first time, I saw that when you commit to any idea, you must ask: Who does that idea exclude? Is there room in this vision of justice for *ubuntu*, for *agape* love, for all of us created equal?

With this realization, as I would discover later, I was still follow-ing in the footsteps of Malcolm X. His lifelong philosophical journey led him to greater intellectual depth and political and spiritual trans-formation. As I learned more about the development of his thinking, I became not just a fan, infatuated with his bold, unbending words, but a philosophical friend. He gave me a new appreciation of nonvio-lence as a tactic.

I have described how the church leadership worried about the re-action among our young people to Joseph's shooting. We were just as concerned for Latanda, Joseph's mother, and what her pain and anger might provoke her to do, what violence she might unleash— not in the streets but on the grieving, frightened, despairing part of herself. After tragedy, those grieving turn inward. Sometimes they do not come out again.

For Latanda, the death of her son was a double blow. First, the unimaginable loss of a child, then the gathering realization that justice was not coming. No witness appeared to reveal who had fired the gun that killed her firstborn. No one claimed the reward our community had offered for information. No arrests were made.

Latanda checked in regularly with the detectives who continued to work on the case, but hope for justice through the legal system faded. She told me, "I found myself going by that spot every month to put some flowers there and to sit. Just to sit and say to myself: My baby lost his life here. His spirit left his body, right here."

None of us learns to restrain our power without help. No one finds the courage and commitment to keep doing so, day after day and night after night, on their own. Latanda was fortunate that she had a community to support her. She explained it to me this way:

It was 10:40 P.M. when we first found out Joseph was gone. My church family heard, and they came out that night, and they have been walking with me ever since. That first Sunday, we were sitting in our usual pew with our extended family, which surprised people because the shooting had been so recent. We were there because that's where we felt the love. That's where we felt most comfortable.

Our church family makes sure they check on me and my other son. They check on my parents as well. They have become like true family—they pray for us; they pray with us. The church deacons constantly tell me they are praying for me. To this very day, members come up to me, telling me they are still praying. They have supported us from the beginning, and there is no end.

Latanda and her remaining son have held marches in Joseph's honor. They have created a scholarship in his name. They find small ways to keep his memory alive, such as wearing buttons with a picture of his face and his childhood name, Jojo. "It's a talking piece," she said. "I'll go into a store and people will say, 'Oh, I know that young man, I've seen him.' They don't always know what to say after that. So I tell them just to say, 'I'm sorry, I'm praying for you.'"

I remember watching TV on the day of the funeral for George Floyd, who died after a white police officer knelt on his neck for eight minutes. Professor Cornel West was interviewed. "What is it about these Black people?" he asked. "So thoroughly subjugated, but they want freedom for everybody." He continued: "I'm not saying we don't have Black thugs and gangsters. I'm talking about the best of our tradition." Professor West went on to wonder why, faced with the Ku Klux Klan, Black Americans did not create their own Black Klan. There could have been "a civil war in every generation, with terror cells in every 'hood." After millions of our people were enslaved, the world might have understood if African Americans had set out, once they got the chance, to destroy their enslavers, burn it all down.

It is a question you could raise about almost any turning point in African American history. What is it about these people and rage? In the 1950s, a fourteen-year-old boy named Emmett Till was beaten and lynched for allegedly speaking in an offensive way to a white woman in a Mississippi grocery store. The woman later admitted she had lied to police about his actions. The killers were acquitted in court. Why did his mother not rage and call on her people to burn all of Mississippi down? Instead, she asked that her boy be buried in an open coffin so that the tens of thousands of mourners could see the brutality of lynching, and perhaps other people's children would not be brutalized like hers.

African Americans have had such experiences in every generation. Yet they created and still sustain the civil rights and Black

Power movements, striving to recognize the humanity of all, even the people who disregard them. There is a depth of spirituality in that choice that is deeper than any doctrine. In that choice, we feel the sacred.

So again, I ask, with Professor West: What is it about these Black people? Why is it that after all we have been through, we are still, mostly, restraining our rage, still demanding that the Constitution of the United States live up to its promises? Black spirituality has been demonstrating to America over and over again the faith that it should have, the deep sacred commitment and practice to redirect our rage and harness our power, whatever our faith. After all of this disregard, we keep bringing something to the table that could save America from itself.

4

Beat Bias

Practice Liberation Listening

> One cannot defend oneself against somebody who is determined
> to prove to himself—not to you but to himself—that you
> are inferior. One has got to walk out of that nightmare.
>
> JAMES BALDWIN

I made my mistake when I was working on a message for a Sunday service. The sermon was meant to lift up Nehemiah, who worked to rebuild Jerusalem in the time of the Second Temple. I wanted to connect his story to the present work of rebuilding the African American community, and specifically to honor African American athletes who have taken a public stand for their principles.

As my media team met to work on the new issue of the bulletin, I asked them to gather photographs of athletes such as Jack Johnson, Jim Brown, and Muhammad Ali. When it was distributed and I delivered my message on Sunday, people seemed to respond well. Afterward, though, when we held our weekly review-of-worship meeting, I heard another point of view.

Minister Jené Colvin, who coordinated our worship and arts

ministries, said, "I opened the bulletin, and I didn't see any women. Where was the WNBA?"

Then I realized. My gosh! The head of media was a guy, the pastor was a guy, and several of the women who were usually part of our planning committee had not been there when we chose the photographs. Without them, the men who remained had been, literally, thoughtless. We did not think about who we were leaving out. Lacking our full planning team, we printed a feature on Black athletes that entirely excluded women.

Of course, I was not new to the idea that women get excluded in the church and in sports, but as a man, hard as I try, there are going to be things that I miss because of my maleness. In my excitement to build a message around my own sports heroes, I had felt completely fine and normal planning a biased bulletin that seemed to treat women athletes as unworthy of being seen or heard.

In my next service for the whole church community, I confessed my bias. I acknowledged what I had allowed to happen. The next week, we featured pictures of women athletes who have taken a stand for what they believed.

That experience reminded me of a scene in *Do the Right Thing*, the Spike Lee movie set in a pizza parlor in Brooklyn. The owner, Sal, who is of Italian heritage, has decorated a wall of his restaurant with photos of famous Italian Americans. Over the years, the neighborhood has become mostly African American, and the story is set in motion when a young Black customer asks the older white man why there are no pictures of famous Black Americans: "Sal," he says, "how come you got no brothers on the wall?"

My bias had cast me in the role of Sal, the one with the fixed doctrine about who deserved to be honored. The women in the congregation were the ones who had to ask, "Hey, Rev., how come you got no sisters in the bulletin?"

In the film, Sal replies angrily that because he owns the business, he will decide whose pictures go on his Wall of Fame. As the story continues, the conflict becomes a physical struggle for raw justice. By the end, a man is dead, and the pizza parlor has been destroyed.

I was also reminded of a different incident of my own bias. In my family, the kids and I have a long-running game of trying to scare each other. The kids will hide behind a door and jump out at me or grab my foot under the dinner table to take me by surprise. I do the same back to them. One day I came into the room where my son, Elijah, was watching television and started talking to him, but he could not hear because he was wearing headphones.

I saw my chance.

I sneaked up behind him and grabbed his shoulder, and he screamed like I was Freddy Krueger and Michael Myers combined.

"You didn't know I was there?" I said to him after he had stopped hollering.

"No, not at all!" he said, and then we both started laughing.

The next day, I was sitting with a group of ministers from a cohort group sponsored by Auburn Seminary in New York City. I told them the story. "You should have heard Elijah," I said. "He started screaming like a girl!"

Two of the ministers who were female looked at each other for a moment. Then they looked at me with similarly ironic smiles.

"Is that a bad thing?" asked one.

"You think only girls get scared?" asked the other. "You think there's something wrong with Elijah showing a little fear?"

Both laughed a little. I understood that they were laughing at me.

I had meant only to describe the way Elijah was hollering in a high-pitched voice, but when they responded as they did, I could hear that there was bias in the way I had said it. I could hear how it could hurt my son too if he heard me talk that way. I could imagine how it could hurt my daughter, my wife, and any woman who respected me.

"You know we love you," one of my minister friends said, "but we're going to correct you."

By combining their love for me with their demand for justice for women, laughing at me but at the same time laughing with me, they helped me to feel the action of justice and love in a single moment.

When the cry for justice comes to us this way, combined with love, it is easier to recognize when we have been participating in bias and exclusion. We may dare to listen to others' perspectives on us, even when they contain criticism, anger, and pain. Ideally, correction would come that way all the time, mixing love with justice. But although we might aspire to call out for justice in the spirit of love, the messy reality is that we often cry out for justice with wailing and with rage. We mean to say "Could you please not leave the lights on when you come to bed?" Instead, we say "You never loved me, you never respected me. I give up!"

We may be adults, but we cry out. We may, under other circumstances, be good at choosing a precise and appropriate vocabulary. When we are in pain, though, especially the searing pain of injustice, we are not. We cannot find the right words. We exaggerate. We accuse. We despair.

That does not mean we were wrong to cry out. It is the responsibility of a person who is hurt to cry out. It is devastating to their spirit and to their development if they muffle the cry and resign themselves to suffering with no end in sight. And so, when we cry out, we are hoping to be heard by someone in whom the power of love is strong.

Someone who has the fearlessness and courage to listen and respond to us, to not turn away and silence us in the middle of our trauma. But very often we are heard by others who are themselves in pain, who are also failing to articulate their experience and their feelings in perfectly precise, fair, and unheated words. And when words and self-control fail them, they have only each other. This is the essential situation of two wronged adults in conflict.

Our deliverance comes when both can listen. Each needs to hear the other crying out; each needs to respond not to the surface accusations or despair but to the underlying source of pain, while at the same time acknowledging their own situation, their own feelings. Listening of this kind—liberation listening—turns dialogue into a spiritual practice. It requires both sides to have faith that if we will truly listen, then your liberation will be my liberation, and mine will contribute to yours.

This spiritual listening can put us in a position of simultaneous vulnerability and possibility, overcoming our biases and habits of exclusion if each side commits to both love and justice. Vulnerability and liberation are cousins. We must listen to one another with the same honesty and compassion that we listen to ourselves. And we must listen to ourselves with the same honesty and compassion we offer to others—even if those others have more power or authority. If one side loves but cannot also insist on equality, we are back to superior and inferior, one who is recognized as fully human and one who is less than. We are back to love without justice. As Malcolm X explained, "Love becomes powerful when you decide to love yourself, and you stand not below or above someone, but on an equal footing, because you have reclaimed your humanity."

As Monica and I have raised our daughter, Makayla, the importance of liberation listening has grown clearer to me. We often talked about how to protect and empower her so that she would not drink the poison crafted by society for girls. In these conversations, it is the duty of a father to listen and become a student of a mother who has a kind of sight not given to all. The best I can do is share the lessons, dreams, and weariness wrapped in Monica's vision of being a child in a world that struggles to affirm being either Black or a woman.

Monica was a child born in the 1970s to young parents blessed to be covered by the cloak of southern sensibilities. She was raised with deep regard for elders, especially the wisdom and ingenuity of women who shaped a life in rural Virginia. In the first half of the twentieth century, a council of elders with a grand matriarch named Johnny Bradley kept a constant vigil over Monica and breathed wisdom into her spirit. Monica saw that these women held sacred knowledge for thriving and navigating a peculiar world.

Monica's parents, children of Virginia, were a son of Buckroe Beach and a daughter of Aberdeen. They later found opportunity at the Kennedy Space Center and the Orlando public schools. But, while their state fancied itself the capital of the Confederacy, their village network, the affirmation of Hampton University, and the discipline of Episcopalian ritual cleared enough dirt off the window of opportunity to allow this couple to imagine a new life.

The wisdom of Monica's elders followed her to Orlando, Florida, where her childhood was framed by a Black Episcopal church and an iconic Bahamian American pastor, Father Nelson Pinder. The experience in Orlando was middle-class and multiethnic, with Afro-Latino, Chinese-Jamaican, and European immigrant families. Yet, with all the diversity and illusion of tranquility, biases of race and gender still cast a shadow on Monica's life.

Her "council of elders"—grandmothers, aunts, and other adopted women of substance—always arrived in her spirit to conjure a deep confidence to help her cast aside this racialized and gendered imagination. Monica has always said, "I knew I was loved. I understood I was sacred, and I walked through my childhood with this sacred feeling." Spelman College offered an academic and cultural frame to claim her humanity. Monica read the works of Toni Morrison, Maya Angelou, and Dr. Johnetta B. Cole, the poets Sonia Sanchez, Pearl Cleage, and Nikki Giovanni, as well as Zora Neale Hurston, Alice Walker, bell hooks, and others, and through their words these authors became her thought partners. Spelman made it clear to many that being a Black woman was a sacred gift.

Our dream is for Makayla to be similarly empowered, yet sensitive to traps designed for girls and young women. She and many in her generation believe in questioning the current order and breaking cultural norms or stereotypes for women. Still, as Monica has noted, the deconstruction of past standards opens the door both for women to be empowered and also for new challenges to arise.

Raising a daughter is tough. We must hear the voice of critique from her lips yet offer the wisdom of the powerful women of her family as guides. We are called to listen and interrogate our bias but also to balance our interpretation with ancient wisdom, older than anything we have ever known.

Listening to others and investigating our biases can lead to an unpredictable series of recognitions and insights. The more we hear, the better we see how we might correct ourselves, our communities, and our nation. Such work is an act of love, whether or not that is immediately recognized. Self-proclaimed patriots often tell protesters, "This is America—love it or leave it!" But it is the spiritual obligation of those who have been marginalized in the space called America to stay, to work, to fight, to criticize and, when necessary, to protest. Inherent in the idea of love is struggle. We must struggle, grapple, and wrestle with the myth, ideal, and truth of America in order to make our union more perfect.

When does it end? When will we discharge our spiritual obligation to listen to others and to question ourselves and our institutions? That day may never come. Even our phones and computers need regular updates. How could beings as miraculously complex as people need less?

Our spiritual experience of our world can never be fully explained, written down, completed. At the very end of his life, Howard Thurman, now many decades past the day he sat down and wept at the train station, gave an interview with the BBC. He said, "Religious experience is dynamic. It's fluid, it's effervescent, it's yeasty. . . . The religious experience goes on experiencing. So whatever creed there is, whatever theology, it's always a little out of date." Our beliefs and our practices, like our proudest institutions, will always be "a little out of date." The work of liberation listening never ends.

5

Rework Your Origin Story

Become a Spiritual Hero

God works through me the same as you. There is
no feat I achieve that you are not capable of.
T'CHALLA, KING OF WAKANDA, *Black Panther*

With everything we've beaten, everything we've endured,
everything we've risen above, everything we've become, no
matter what comes next, we've won. We've already won.
RICK GRIMES, *The Walking Dead*

There is something in us, as storytellers and as listeners to
stories, that demands the redemptive act, that demands that
what falls at least be offered the chance to be restored.
FLANNERY O'CONNOR

Ever since I was a kid, I have wondered where heroes come from. How
some people, bruised and broken, find ways to not just tolerate the
darkness and seize opportunities in the chaos, but to transform themselves and do extraordinary good. How some nations do the same.

I first found stories of transformation like that in my comic books. The origin stories of so many superheroes begin when they are lost and miserable. The baby who would become Superman was born to parents whose world was about to be destroyed. They placed their child alone in a spacecraft to Earth, where he arrived as a helpless orphan, knowing no one.

Storm, the mutant hero of the X-Men franchise, lost her parents in Egypt during a war. She survived on the city streets as a homeless thief. Like the young Superman, she saw evidence that she could do things others could not—her thoughts and feelings influenced the weather—but she did not know how to develop those gifts or what purpose they might serve.

Rick Grimes from *The Walking Dead* was an ordinary family man and police officer who was knocked unconscious in the line of duty. Then the zombies started walking, and he woke up alone in his hospital bed, unable to contact anyone he knew and desperate to survive as society collapsed around him.

Any of these three might have been defeated by such harsh events. They might have described themselves something like this: *I am a victim of circumstances in a world that is dangerous, cruel, and unjust. I can't trust or depend on others. I have no moral code beyond looking out for myself. I do what I must to survive.* That is the essence of their stories when we meet them.

With their bitter pasts, hunger to survive, and unique physical powers, they might easily have become possessed by the demon of self-centeredness, only ever out for themselves. They might have become villains. In fact, if you compare the origin stories of heroes and villains, you will find they begin in similar ways. The humbling aspect of our origins is that we are all potentially heroes and villains, saints and sinners, protagonists and antagonists, until we begin to make choices.

For each of these three I mentioned, events unfolded to offer new and dramatic alternatives for understanding themselves and their place in the world. The orphaned boy who didn't know he could be Superman was found and taken in by a childless human couple who raised him. There are different versions of Superman's origin stories from different comic-book series, television shows, and movies, but the essential parts are the same: His adoptive parents care for him and help him learn to control his powers and use them for good. They bring him into the loving circle of a larger community. He finds a way to be part of society (as Clark Kent) and a way to use the powerful gifts he was given on behalf of society in the service of a greater moral code.

Dramatic events also offer Storm a choice: When the young woman wanders into Africa's Serengeti desert, she meets a priestess who becomes a second mother to her and teaches her to harness her powers. Rick Grimes, meanwhile, is an ordinary human with no special powers—not an obvious candidate to be a superhero—yet he faces a superhuman struggle. At first, his only goals are to save himself and to find his wife and son. Soon, however, he meets others struggling to not only survive but to keep their humanity as civility, faith, and love crumble around them. He discovers that although he is an ordinary man, his police training and his natural gifts make him exceptionally good at fighting the evils of his place and time. (In this way, Rick is a bit like Batman.)

What fascinates me about these characters is not just that former victims discover they have unusual powers or that they become crime fighters. Their comic-book transformations from victim to superhero hide a spiritual mystery. Like Clark Kent in a phone booth, these characters remake themselves, taking on a new and more authentic identity, and they become powerful and purposeful in ways no one would have expected. Isn't that what we all wish to do?

Instead of continuing her solitary life as a thief, Storm joins the X-Men to fight evil and become a leader and nurturer of other young, lost mutants, a beacon of power and calm. Rick Grimes intends to fight only for himself and his immediate family, yet in time he makes the choice to fight for the whole human family. These victims bent only on their own survival find a higher purpose, a spiritual perspective on their troubled world, and opportunities to make that world better.

As I grew up, reading and watching stories of superheroes in a home that also lifted up the tradition of Dr. King, I made the connection. Before their transformations, these characters' lives were incomplete in Dr. King's sense. Love and justice were out of balance in all three dimensions. They had not achieved the authentic fulfillment of the self because they did not yet know what gifts they had been given, how to use them, or what a meaningful use of those gifts might be. Lacking community, they had not developed their sense of engagement and social responsibility. And they had no relationship to spirituality or God, beyond sometimes wishing for divine help when they got into trouble. In their transformations, however, they remade themselves and their relationships both on Earth and with the spiritual, becoming embodiments of love linked to justice.

Then I made another discovery: Such people exist. They do not have X-ray vision or the power to cause thunder and lightning (as far as I know), but their courageous transformations and community-changing skills are equally inspiring. Consider the deacons at my church. Some of our most important spiritual caregivers, they are dispatched whenever loss or trauma tears at our community. They visit the sick, attend funerals, and lead prayer groups. They serve Communion. Honored and treasured, they are heroes we rely on at the hardest of times. So it boggled my mind to learn how many of our deacons had spent years in the darkness fighting spiritual demons. So many had stories that began, like Storm's, far from the heroic. Hearing of their past trauma, addiction, moral lapses, and, sometimes, incarceration, it was almost like encountering two different people, the "before" character and the "after" character. How, I wondered, had these seemingly broken people transformed themselves into community heroes?

Had you met Donna Hammond at age sixty, you would have been privileged to speak with a forty-five-year member of our church, a deacon for fifteen years, who was studying in seminary to become a minister herself. The church's media projects manager, Donna was a published author, the proud mother of two, and the grandmother of nine. That is the "after" picture.

Now check her out "before." From the age of about six, as she has described in her published writings, she was sexually molested by her mother's boyfriend, who later became her stepfather. The abuse continued until she finally told her brother when she was a teenager. He told her mother, who called Donna into her bedroom to stand in front of her abuser and repeat what she had said.

Confronted with his crimes, her stepfather denied everything. Donna's mother chose to believe her husband, and the mother-daughter relationship became badly strained. Donna told me, "My mother didn't tell me she loved me, didn't wrap me in her arms. We weren't close. You read in Scripture about how parents train up a child, but I was not trained up like that."

Against her mother's wishes, Donna moved in with her grandmother. Around that time, she fell deeply in love with a young man who returned her feelings but was too immature to become her life partner. Then he got her pregnant, and Donna's grandmother passed away at about the same time. Donna's mother moved her daughter, now six months pregnant, back into her childhood home, under the same roof as her abuser.

For the next few unhappy years, Donna had a variety of partners as she traded sex for the illusion of caring. She felt like a broken vessel, damaged goods, and she lived with a deep distrust of men and authority. She had no regular work and no vision of her own future. Statistically, as a survivor of child sexual abuse, she was likely to wind up with a life of failed relationships, drug and alcohol abuse, compulsive promiscuity, and the possibility that she might become a sexual predator herself. She on her way to becoming a villain.

One oasis in those hard teenage years was a friend next door whose family went to church. Donna started attending with them on Sundays just to get out of the house and be with her friend. She found to her surprise that she felt welcome at church, even happy. "People have this way of looking down on you when they feel you are broken," she told me, but "at this church, no one judged me, not the pastor and not the deacons. Even if people didn't say 'I'm here for you,' I felt support in what they *didn't* say. They didn't say 'What's wrong with you? You're sleeping around! You're having babies with no husband!'"

Based on her experience with men, Donna was distrustful of the pastor at that time, a man named Jeremiah Wright. "I had seen elders talk to children any kind of way, disrespectful. Teens can be disrespectful as well—they're not angels—but there is a code that makes some elders feel they can speak to youth and young adults any way they want, degrading and diminishing people, negating their voice. But Pastor Wright was always one who believes everyone should have a voice. He took an interest in our interests.

"At that time on Sundays, the choir sang anthems and hymns of the church, but some of us younger people wanted to sing gospel. And we were good! Pastor Wright allowed us to get involved in the worship experience, and it was more than just letting us do a special gospel program on Easter Sunday. He let us get involved in the ministry of the church, join the leadership council, and become youth representatives for the Illinois conference."

The church community and Pastor Wright were giving Donna the chance to challenge her origin story. She had felt defined by her victimization, a woman too damaged for an elder to treat respectfully or a man to love. In church, though, she began to tell herself a different story. Treated with respect, she began to see in herself what the church people saw: a talented, valuable member of the community with gifts to contribute. She was building what Dr. King called a more complete life.

"I stayed here in church," Donna explained. "I worked here, I participated in the scouting program here. I kept busy, got involved, and, in time, became a facilitator for teens. So many of these kids need love more than anything. You may see them around, looking like normal kids, but you don't realize they're not getting love at home."

Despite her pain, Donna kept off drugs and off the streets. Slowly, with her encouragement, her entire family joined the church, bringing them closer together again. Donna continued to thrive. When her older son was grown, he went looking for his father, the caring but immature young man who had been Donna's one true love. When the young man found him, he put his parents back in touch. They were more mature now, but their feelings had not changed, and, in their fifties, the couple finally married.

Through her church family, Donna had come to see her past differently and, with it, her nature. She no longer told her own story as that of a hopelessly damaged victim of abuse. She was a child of God, recognized as such by her church family, a person worthy of love and possessed of gifts to share; and in her work as a church deacon ministering to at-risk young people, she became a local hero. She had remade her relationship to God, to her community, and to herself. To me, Donna's transformation to her more complete life is as amazing as a newspaper reporter who puts on a cape and flies into the air.

However, Superman in a phone booth may not be the most helpful comparison for human beings from Earth who want to find their heroism. First, when you look around the streets today, you will not find many phone booths, especially not the kind with the doors that close. It is a running gag in the Superman movies that he has nowhere to change clothes. Second, and more spiritually, transformation from victim to hero is not something you accomplish in private. The heroic transformations that I am talking about happen not alone but through our relationships.

I think of Deacon Lawrence Myles, twenty years sober as I write this, who once struggled with alcoholism. His disease came between him and his children because he was too drunk or too focused on getting his next drink to show up for them. One day his daughter was in the hospital, and he tried to pull himself together to visit her. She was the one who was sick, but when he got to her hospital room, he was drunk, weeping and crying so much that finally he had to find a bathroom where he could pull himself together. He tells the story of how he reached for a paper towel, and in the reflection of the metal towel dispenser he saw his own face. The image was warped and misshapen in the uneven metal, but he could make out his bloodshot, teary eyes, the wet mess from his nose, and he felt: *My God, that's who I am. That misshapen thing is my soul. I never want to see myself that way again. That's not who my daughter needs.*

Deacon Myles promised himself then that he would remember that moment. He would no longer be defined to the world as the disappointment who did what the bottle told him to do. He would become the hero he was called to be: a reliable father for his children.

Of course, one moment of resolution does not change anyone. There was hard work to be done. Deacon Myles went into a rehab program, got sober, and now sees a very different man in the bathroom mirror, in part because he has never forgotten the misshapen image he saw that day. This is a heroic choice. As the poet Mary Oliver writes in her poem "The Journey":

> One day you finally knew
> what you had to do, and began,
> though the voices around you
> kept shouting
> their bad advice—
> though the whole house
> began to tremble
> and you felt the old tug
> at your ankles.
> "Mend my life!"
> each voice cried.
> But you didn't stop.
> You knew what you had to do,
> though the wind pried
> with its stiff fingers
> at the very foundations,
> though their melancholy
> was terrible.
> It was already late
> enough, and a wild night,
> and the road full of fallen
> branches and stones.
> But little by little,

as you left their voices behind,

the stars began to burn

through the sheets of clouds,

and there was a new voice

which you slowly

recognized as your own,

that kept you company

as you strode deeper and deeper

into the world,

determined to do

the only thing you could do—

determined to save

the only life you could save.

The impulse to transform ourselves is a private demand for justice. We rise up and say, first of all, to ourselves: *This is wrong. I was not meant for this. I was not created to be a victim, an addict, a second-class citizen, a disappointment. I must be treated with dignity, recognized for my gifts and not just for my failings.* Those are demands for justice. But the transformation that justice requires must be nourished by love. We find the inspiration and the means to change our stories in our relationships. Deacon Myles saw himself differently because he looked at himself through his daughter's eyes. Donna Hammond reconsidered her cruel self-judgments because her church community saw more potential in her than she did in herself. Our heroes get knocked down and pick themselves up again to fight for justice, yes, but they do so under the gaze of love.

To rewrite our origin stories, we need to look at our past with a perspective of grace. We must acknowledge our failings while looking for the elements that we can consecrate and remix. Not only individuals, but families, communities, and nations can rewrite an origin story. The author Marilynne Robinson has observed that the Constitution of the United States is one of the world's greatest works of fiction. When the "founding fathers" wrote in the Declaration of Independence: "We hold these truths to be self-evident, that all men are created equal," they were not stating a scientific fact. They were telling a new story, not yet reflected in the laws and institutions of any country. Not even in the United States, where slavery was legal, women lacked a long list of rights, and only white men with property could participate in politics. The founders proposed a new story for their new country, saying: *We must live by the recognition that we were all made by the same Creator, a Creator who created us equal. The evidence is right before you—just look.* That truth might have been self-evident, but truths still need heroes to fight for them. Fighting for the equality of all became part of the new country's spiritual origin story—not our condition, then, but the conclusion toward which we would work.

Outside of communities of faith, too many miss that essential element, spirit. Rewriting our origin stories in America, as individuals and as a nation, was from the beginning a spiritual matter. We rewrote and are still rewriting our national origin story by engaging with the divine because the "founding fathers" traced our inalienable human rights to our creation, our source. This does not make us a Christian nation, as some suggest, but those founders who borrowed philosophical ideals from indigenous communities, used stolen labor, and denied full agency to women stumbled serendipitously upon a spiritual ideal that all humanity, across geography and faiths, must face.

That engagement with the divine was crucial to the future Rev. Dr. Martin Luther King Jr. He needed to rewrite his own origin story before he could do the same for his people and his country. Born just before the start of the Depression, with Jim Crow still casting a heavy shadow over the dreams of children of color, he was witness to a full share of hardship and injustice around him. Yet he was able to find what he needed to inoculate himself against the larger narrative of racial caste and racial hate, and to lift up a different story of what America can be.

To understand how Dr. King revised his origin story, we need to look closely at his place of origin. The state of Georgia was born between the dream of social reform and the afflictions of the plantation economy, between the values of noble optimism and the curse of unrestricted greed. The final colony to be formed in the "New World," Georgia was the only one governed by a board of trustees based in England. Upon the birth of the settlement in Savannah, slavery was explicitly outlawed—along with rum, lawyers, and Catholics. James Oglethorpe, one of the twenty-one trustees, believed Georgia could be a space for redemption, where prisoners could be dispatched to work off debts to the Crown. Land would be allotted by the trustees to inmates as a form of restorative justice, allowing them to build a life above the poverty line while paying off their debts to the monarchy. Oglethorpe's vision was overruled for the sake of a quicker return on the monarchy's investment in its new colony, but the spirit of his idea lingered in the soil of Georgia. Georgia became a haven for working people who created "the city too busy to hate," called Atlanta. Black farmhands, domestics, and former slaves became barbers and rail workers, a growing middle class that believed in racial uplift through protest, entrepreneurship, and education.

The epicenter of this socioeconomic resistance was the Fourth Ward of Atlanta, east of downtown, known as Auburn Avenue, or "Sweet Auburn." There, in the generation before Dr. King, three men collaborated to improve the economic and spiritual well-being of people of African descent. The first was Alonzo Herndon, a person of mixed racial heritage who, though born into the institution of slavery, nevertheless carried around within him a divine arrogance. He believed he was created by God and as good as anyone. He left the sharecropping plantation with only one year of formal schooling and eleven dollars in his pocket, and he learned the barber trade, eventually opening his own shop. Success led him to open two more locations, one for an exclusive, downtown white clientele.

In his shop for white folks, Herndon used the arrogance and ignorance of racism to his advantage. Many of his elite clients never thought a "colored" man was smart enough to eavesdrop and use the intel he overheard to build his own economic empire. Herndon quietly listened to his powerful clients and absorbed their business acumen, then created the Atlanta Life Insurance Company on Auburn Avenue. Not only did it make him Atlanta's first Black millionaire, but it was also an early form of cooperative racial uplift economics.

The second man was Rev. William Holmes Borders, a preacher born in Macon, Georgia. He studied what is today called the "Black Social Gospel" at Morehouse College and became the pastor of the Wheat Street Baptist Church on Auburn. Reverend Borders distinguished himself as a civil rights leader in the city of Atlanta, partnering with John Wesley Dobbs, the unofficial "mayor of Black Atlanta," on several voting rights campaigns. Borders, Dobbs, and Herndon together were able to organize sections of the Black community into a power base that pressured Mayor William Hartsfield to hire Black police officers and bus drivers, again expanding the city's middle class.

Reverend Borders's oratory was legendary; he stood over six-four with a powerful voice, poetic prose, and an unapologetically Black theology. I can imagine a fourteen-year-old Black boy in Atlanta named Martin King who felt a call to become a minister and often sneaked into the back of Wheat Street Baptist. There he heard this powerful preacher tell the congregation about a God of justice who loved Black people. He saw Reverend Borders portray Jesus as a tall, powerful Black man in a citywide Easter production that refuted all the assumptions of Jim Crow segregation. He began to dream.

Reverend Borders often stood in his pulpit reciting a poem he had penned titled "I Am Somebody," later remixed by Rev. Jesse Jackson as a call-and-response to encourage students struggling in under-funded schools in the South. I can picture young Martin King sitting in the rear of the church absorbing the words of Reverend Borders:

I am somebody—

I am a poet in Langston Hughes.
I am an author in Frank Yerby.
I am a creator of rhyme in Paul Laurence Dunbar.
I am a Christian Statesman in J.R.E. Lee
I am a diplomat in Ralph A. Bunche . . .

In this thriving Black neighborhood where economic, social, and spiritual uplift were all possible and on display, the future Rev. Dr. Martin Luther King Jr. found a model of the future for not just Atlanta but for America, a national life remade in all its dimensions. With that new origin story in mind, the future spiritual superhero set to work.

6

Practice Prophetic Grief

Forgive to Build Spiritual Resistance

Resentment is like drinking poison and then
hoping it will kill your enemies.

NELSON MANDELA

Forgiveness is a virtue of the brave.

INDIRA GANDHI

It was a June night in 2015 when a young white man, twenty-one years of age, walked into the church in Charleston, South Carolina, known as Mother Emanuel, one of the oldest and most revered Black churches in the South. The pastor was conducting Bible study when the young man sat down next to him and joined the conversation. As the other worshippers began to pray, he unzipped his fanny pack, removed a handgun loaded with hollow-core bullets designed to do maximum harm, and opened fire. He killed nine people, six women and three men.

The shooter, Dylann Roof, fled the church but was captured by police the next morning. He confessed to planning the attack as an expression of his hatred, views that matched posts on his website expressing hostility to people he categorized as "blacks," "Hispanics," "Jews," and "East Asians." He told the police he had no relationship to the people he killed or to the church where he committed murder. His goal was to provoke all African Americans to violence. He wanted, he said, "to start a race war."

Such horrors claw at our spirit. How can we face them? How do we respond?

News of the massacre sparked national outrage. The authorities placed a million-dollar bond on the shooter's head. Public debate focused on questions of punishment: How severe? How soon? Was a lifetime in prison enough? The governor of South Carolina called for prosecutors to seek the death penalty. For at least a little while, there was a shared feeling of national outrage at this inhuman crime.

Only two days later, at Roof's bond hearing, some of the survivors of the attack and some family members of the murdered victims spoke to the killer through a video link. They wanted to talk to him directly. What, you have to wonder, could they have felt at that moment? Did they want to scream out their rage and grief? Did they want the satisfaction of seeing the monster in chains, afraid for his life?

In this public setting, something unexpected happened. Far from screaming out their hate and pain, several grieving mothers, fathers, and children of the murdered offered forgiveness to the murderer. They redirected their rage, as I described in chapter three, but they went further. The daughter of victim Ethel Lance said about her mother, "I will never talk to her ever again. I will never be able to hold her again." And then she said to Roof, "But I forgive you and have mercy on your soul. You hurt me. You hurt a lot of people. May God forgive you, and I forgive you."

When these expressions of mercy spread in the media, some felt shocked. Was it right to forgive a crime so terrible? In what way, commentators asked, did a cold-blooded killer who dreamed of war between the races deserve a pardon?

The answer is that Roof did not deserve it. Mercy is only mercy when someone is guilty. Grace is only grace when it's unwarranted, the thing you should not receive, yet receive anyway. Mercy and grace are part of the African American church tradition but, even so, some prominent African American writers objected. The professor and essayist Roxane Gay tweeted that she did not remember any movement to forgive ISIS for their beheadings. Why talk about forgiving white terrorists, she asked, when we do not forgive brown ones? She questioned the motives of those who praised the Black families who forgave the killer. Later, she wrote: "What white people are really asking for when they demand forgiveness from a traumatized community is absolution." She was pointing to the long history of the call to forgive being used against the marginalized, placing an additional burden on those already most burdened. White nationalists kill African Americans, African Americans forgive, white nationalists kill again.

In personal conversations, I heard from plenty of people who were, like the victims' families, "churchgoing" African Americans. They seemed to lack a spiritual context for these offers of forgiveness. How could those heartsick survivors, family members, and friends bring themselves to do it, especially so soon? Did they not hunger for revenge?

I believe they did hunger. I suspect we have all felt that hunger. Neurologists tell us that revenge satisfies the same parts of the brain that are stimulated by eating. The old expression says "Revenge is a dish best served cold." (Or, as Tony Soprano put it, "Revenge is like serving cold cuts.") So, yes, I get that hunger. And I see that many of our movies and television shows celebrate it. They promise that vengeance will feed us, becoming our satisfaction and our empowerment. The hero with gun in hand will surprise the villain and open fire. Who does not feel the drama and satisfaction of vengeance?

Retribution feeds our hunger, yes—but not for long. In the moment, violent action feels like taking power, correcting an injustice; but even when vengeance is deserved, it does not set things right. I say this not to make a moral judgment but to state a practical fact. As Dr. King described in his sermon "Where Do We Go from Here?" there is a practical limit to what violent retribution can do for us. "Through violence you may murder a murderer," he wrote, "but you can't murder murder. Through violence you may murder a liar, but you can't establish truth. Through violence you may murder a hater, but you can't murder hate through violence."

Had Dylann Roof simply been born bad, an isolated outbreak of the disease of evil, an anomaly, then perhaps the solution would have been to destroy him like a rabid dog. Society could catch and kill him, feel better, and get back to normal, rid of his threat forever. This was the spirit of that moment of angry unity that seemed to follow his arrest, the united call for punishment. Coming together in anger can feel good, for a while. But while the nation soothed itself in shared outrage about one murderer, while the media helped us to narrow our vision to focus on one evil act, we looked away from that lost young man's spiritual parents. We neglected his history and our own. We could see what had happened before but not what would happen again. In this way, the country's united rage at Dylann Roof became a convenient distraction from a deeper spiritual challenge.

Dylann Roof, unfortunately, was no exceptional outbreak of evil. That twenty-one-year-old brother was not even born bad. I think of the old show tune that says "You've got to be taught before it's too late . . . to hate all the people your relatives hate!" Dylann Roof had been *taught*. So, although he was the agent of the Charleston church massacre, he was not the deep source of the hatred and harm.

How was he taught? He never finished high school, but he received a full education in race hatred, an affliction that diminishes the soul. His schooling drew from established sources. Online, he read and wrote admiringly about the failed apartheid regimes of the former Rhodesia and South Africa. He posed for a picture on his website with a gun and a Confederate flag, celebrating the violent fight to maintain the institution of slavery. That young man studied the world's worst examples of institutionalized hatred, drinking in a long tradition of racist miseducation. Because of that tradition, we have met Dylann Roof many times in the long struggle for freedom. Because of that tradition, we will meet him again, many times, in the future.

The media gave us a long close-up on the villain as if he were an exceptional character, but if we imagine pulling back from that dramatic close-up, we can see not just the shooter but the place that shaped him. Widening the angle, we take in the city of Charleston, South Carolina, where the horrific shooting took place. Charleston is a great city, but for all its beauty and wonder, it has struggled to deal with the scars of its history. Forty percent of all Africans who came to America in chains came through Charleston. The trade in human flesh made Charleston, before Reconstruction, the wealthiest city in America. It was in Charleston that the shots rang out that started the Civil War.

However, I do not mean to put all the blame for shaping Dylann Roof on South Carolina. The state was itself formed as a part of the South, a region where so many Americans who were not enslaved flourished thanks to the stolen labor of those who were. After emancipation, in the Reconstruction era, the South was rebuilt through conscripted, unpaid Black labor. New laws criminalized actions as minor as jaywalking, breaking curfew, and gathering in groups of more than two or three. The inmates of the swelling prison population were sold to white companies that required prisoners to work off their sentences. These policies, and others blocking African Americans from inheriting land and voting, wove a web of inhuman restriction that covers the South to this day.

And the South, of course, is a part of the United States, an entire nation where the factories flourished as they manufactured the raw materials produced by slaves; where the port cities thrived because of the profitable trade in those raw materials and those factory products and those enslaved people themselves; and where racist policies and practices in education, real estate, banking, policing, and other areas still wait to be redressed.

When we widen our view to take in the history of this country, a country that enshrined in its Constitution the original sins of slavery and the destruction of the Indigenous peoples, we see at last why we are fated to meet Dylann Roof again, no matter how many times we catch and kill him. Far from being one mad dog, one unthinkably ugly anomaly, he is a person whose dark acts grew out of the darkness that has shadowed America from its genesis. That darkness is expressed today, according to the Southern Poverty Law Center, in the record numbers of hate groups—over one thousand separate organizations—now active across this country, targeting Black and brown people, immigrants, LGBTQ people, and women, among others. We live in a time when some Americans think it is acceptable to talk about slavery as if it were a job opportunity, a time when some Americans in their talk and actions and policies elevate the fascism of Nazi Germany. But the goals of these groups are also served by policies and legislation that do not speak in the familiar terms of hate, such as the marijuana drug laws that have led since the Nixon era to the incarceration of so many young men of color. The ideas of these groups have seeped into our civic conversation and behavior. That old, hateful impulse toward race war is not gone but hidden, like a poison with no taste that has been added to the water supply.

At the same time that these ideas have spread, we have also become the world's greatest gun buyers, gun sellers, gun traders, and gun worshippers, and all that firepower makes it easy for those compelled by hate and fear to wreak havoc. Under these conditions, a few lost young men get so drunk on the wine of Confederate supremacy, so high on the opium of race hatred, that they commit unimaginable acts. But the underlying toxic conditions and hateful traditions are what corrupt those few lost young men who become our Dylann Roofs.

To rid ourselves of all of them—not just this racist terrorist or future racist terrorists, but all the destructive racists, whatever tools they use—we need a fresh response to violent tragedy. No death sentence nor series of death sentences for the perpetrators will stop the disease from being transmitted. Nor will we change this country with emotional expressions of our hurt and outrage or earnest pleas to come together as one. It is necessary to acknowledge and express our pain and our hopes for the future, but those expressions will not suffice to reshape a nation.

For the same reason, we must not allow poorly articulated, shallow, and false definitions of forgiveness to trip us up just as we are getting on a better path. So let me explain what forgiveness is not. By "forgiveness," I do not mean that old advice to "forgive and forget." I do not mean holding hands and singing "Kumbaya" and forgetting the scars, the bruises, the bullet holes and broken bones. It does not mean that all of us should come together briefly, ignore history, and celebrate an illusion of community reconciliation, then get back to business as usual. Dr. King said in his sermon "Loving Your Enemies": "Forgiveness does not mean ignoring what has been done or putting a false label on an evil act." It is poison to be asked to forgive and forget. We must acknowledge what has been done, remember it, and refuse to accept it either this time or in the future.

As Ta-Nehisi Coates has argued, it is a false choice either to forgive or to take revenge. "Even if nonviolence isn't always the answer, King reminds us to work for a world where it is. Part of that work is recognizing when our government can credibly endorse King's example. Sparing the life of Dylann Roof would be such an instance." Neither "forgive and forget" nor revenge makes the world any different. The same nightmare will return on another night.

To practice *spiritual resistance* after we have suffered a loss or an assault, we have to make a different choice. The choice is in *how* we grieve. Do we grieve *pathetically*, meaning that we express our pathos, our suffering and emotion? Of course, those expressions of pain or anger are necessary and real, but they are not enough. They may give us moments of cathartic outrage or tears, but they fail to offer true resistance and liberation. Pathetic grief acknowledges our suffering, but it does nothing to change those forces in the world that gave rise to that suffering.

We must learn to grieve *prophetically*, seeing our world, even at its darkest, with the spirit and energy of the prophets of the Hebrew Bible. Those ancient teachers warned that the world was out of balance and that its repair requires our help. Grieving with them, we weep sometimes, yes, but without giving in to cynicism, hatred, and violence. We mourn as we work for change.

The universe is structured with several simple spiritual principles, one being that what you sow, you shall reap. In the Book of Proverbs, we are warned: "Envy not the oppressor and do not copy any of his ways." When we grieve pathetically, we may come to imitate our oppressors, taking our revenge by answering outrage with outrage, violence with violence. We ignore the warning of the poet Audre Lorde: "The master's tools will never dismantle the master's house."

This is as true of small losses and injuries as it is of large ones. Imagine that a member of my extended family regularly insults my cooking. When I show up at a family gathering with a New Orleans style dish or with an African recipe I was excited to share, I get the same speech, in front of everyone. They say I ought to "cook some normal food that people want to eat." This makes me feel bad about having shown up at all. I could express my hurt feelings, my grief, by telling the person off, getting a little revenge by insulting something that they do. Or maybe I could plant a little malicious story about them with another family member. Or maybe I could try to "forgive and forget," but experience has already shown me that while I may forget about it until the next time, when they come at me again with the same complaints, I will feel hurt again, angry again, and those injuries tend to build up over time.

None of those possible responses would create any change. None would work to make our relationship or our whole family community thrive. I would do better to try to be like the Hebrew prophets and consider: What keeps getting us into this painful situation? What could we do together to stay out of it?

Maybe I could call that person up a few days before the next family gathering and say, "You know what? I'm looking forward to seeing you this weekend. It's been a minute. But could I ask you something? When I come in with whatever dish I'm going to cook, would you do me a favor and not say anything about it until the folks who want to try it get to have a taste?" If I said something like that, I would still be expressing my grief, but I would be doing it in a way that sees a better future. That is what makes it prophetic.

The challenge is to remember, even in our justified hurt and anger, that answering insult with insult and harm with harm just worsens the situation for everyone. We must remember the words of Dr. King: "Darkness cannot put out darkness; only light can do that." When we grieve prophetically, we heal ourselves and the world by looking to shape the larger forces that damaged the soul of the person who caused hurt or anger, whether minor or devastating. Like the friends and families of the victims of Dylann Roof, we understand that while he did evil, he was not the root of that evil.

To get to the root of evil, remember the words of Ephesians: "We are not fighting against humans. We are fighting against forces and authorities and against rulers of darkness and powers in the spiritual world" (Eph. 6:12 CEV). In other words, we must resist the tendency to let our differences, whether small differences about food or the biggest differences of politics, turn us against one person or one group of people. Ask instead: How could I live my spiritual values? How could I be part of a change in this home, this community, this nation, or this world that makes it truer to the divine spark within us all?

That choice is not easy to make. Acts of hatred, brutality, and terror, even many acts of plain old meanness, are purposeful. Part of their purpose is to dominate their victims—not just physically but psychologically; not just in the moment of the attack but through trauma that lasts. This is the method of the schoolyard bully and of the terrorist or dictator. Perpetrators of acts of brutality want the taste to linger with their victims every single day, so their victims' lives become defined by the outrages and the violence done to them. Dylann Roof said as much to the police. The goal of his violent spree was not nine deaths, it was ongoing war between people of different races—an enduring relationship of hate and harm. A poison for our souls.

You might think that the only response to a relationship of hate and harm is to get out of that relationship, but escape is not always simple. As human beings, we have no choice but to live in relationship with one another. That is how we were created. Our only choice is what *kind* of relationships we live in. When we become stuck in pathetic grief, we sink into despair or burn night and day for revenge. We have chosen a relationship of fighting, inwardly, all the time, crying all the time, hating all the time: an inward war. It is as if anger, fear, and the fantasy of vengeance chain us to our enemy, and in that hellish struggle, we drag them with us wherever we go. It is exhausting. If we choose to fight in that kind of conflict, we have already given victory to the darkness, because fighting our war becomes our whole world.

What can stop that endless war? Forgiveness—if forgiveness is part of prophetic grief. Not a gift the victim gives the victimizer, but a grace that victims offer themselves, to break the chains that bind them to the ones who did them harm. In offering forgiveness, we say: *Enough! I am so much more than the harm you did. The Creation is more than the evil you do. Your violence took a piece of my soul, but I won't give you the rest. Your actions will not define my world, determine my future, or limit my destiny.*

The survivors and family members of those murdered by Dylann Roof offered him forgiveness not because he deserved it, not because they were ready to forget, not to absolve white people for the long history of racist violence, but to get free. They chose not to accept the role he tried to force on them, as perpetual enemies in a race war. Although they had lost loved ones, although their spirits had been bruised, they affirmed the end to his power. That murderer would not also steal their beliefs, their gifts. He could not make them waste their lives in seeking vengeance. They chose to cut him loose and to keep the imagination that shows a better way, a better future.

We forgive not as a gift of absolution for the victimizer but as resistance against the spiritual infections of despair, vengeance, and chaos. We still seek accountability for evil acts, but we forgive in our hearts so we can better serve the best ideals of our community and our nation. In forgiveness, we remember Psalm 139, in which the Psalmist celebrates being a child of God:

> For You created my inmost being;
> You knit me together in my mother's womb.
> I praise You because I am fearfully and wonderfully made;
> Your works are wonderful,
> I know that full well.

When we remember how we are made—fearfully, wonderfully— we remember how much more we are than any crime committed against us. We see how much more we have been given than any loss we have suffered. Then we may discover that we can forgive not by diminishing ourselves, not by giving in, but by being true to our divine nature. Our miraculous nature can never be taken from us. Think of the Book of Romans: "Neither death nor life, neither angels nor demons, neither the present nor the future, nor any powers, neither height nor depth nor anything else in all creation will be able to separate us from the love of God."

Even so, as I said earlier, it is not easy to choose to forgive. It is hard to admit when our lives have gotten tangled in an ongoing inner relationship with the very person or people who have hurt us most.

To offer forgiveness to those who do not in any sense deserve to be forgiven can seem too much to ask. Dr. King said forgiveness means "that the evil act no longer remains as a barrier to the relationship. Forgiveness is a catalyst creating the atmosphere necessary for a fresh start and a new beginning." Often, though, we feel we do not want any relationship with the person who has done us harm. We do not want any fresh start. We may feel we have lost so much, given up so much, we cannot also grant forgiveness.

And yet, even those people who commit the most demonic acts are not wholly demons. Not even the shooter from the Charleston church massacre. He was born into the world like the rest of us, as someone's baby. The hope of his mother and father was not to raise a mass murderer. His racist training went against his spiritual nature, as I could hear in something he said at his confession. When he walked into the church and sat down to share in Bible worship, he explained, he could hardly go through with his terrible plan because, he said, "Everyone there was so nice to me." In that statement, I hear the lonely, frightened, horribly confused and damaged young man still wishing for love, the young man who let himself get swallowed by the monster of racism. I sense the unextinguished light of the divine in him, despite it all.

I believe the divine seeks to live through us. The universe is inspired to birth our redemption, and we can tell that is so because we were created as extraordinary beings with astonishing potential. It is up to us to choose to make use of those gifts we have been given, fearfully and wonderfully, even at those times when all we can see is darkness.

Even in *The Art of War*, the military strategist Sun Tzu advised that a general should never operate out of revenge because revenge clouds judgment. Even in war! He recommended treating the enemy well, so that they will consider converting to your cause. He wrote that it was foolish to punish the children of soldiers of the opposing army because their grandchildren and great-grandchildren will come back seeking to destroy the punisher. This legendary military general made it clear that vengeance is bad not just as a moral matter but *bad military tactics for the avenger* because it makes it harder to win the real war. And that is our spiritual goal too: winning the real war, rooting out the evil in our personal lives, our communities, and our nation.

As Dr. King reminded us even during the triumphs of the freedom movement in the 1960s, "The plant of freedom has grown only a bud and not yet a flower." A bud is a wondrous thing, a miracle, a sign of hope for the future. Farmers can feel justifiably proud to see buds on the trees in their orchards. But a bud is not a flower, a flower is not yet a fruit, and even with the moments of beauty we may witness in our personal lives and in our nation, the work of spiritual resistance is far from done.

7

Pardon Our Dust

Meet Failings with Grace

From dust you came, to dust you shall return.

ECCLESIASTES 3:20

If you forgive others the wrongs they have done

to you, your God will also forgive you.

MATTHEW 6:14

Love is holy because it is like grace—the worthiness

of its object is never really what matters.

MARILYNNE ROBINSON, *Gilead*

I received an urgent phone call from the family of a girl I'll call Terri, a senior, honor-roll student at a Chicago public high school. Active at Trinity Church her entire life, Terri was a leader in several youth ministries, known for her power to charm almost anyone she met. In her senior year, already accepted to several excellent colleges, she met a boy she found funny and attractive, and she charmed him as well. They started dating.

Her new boyfriend spent too much time getting high and was even known occasionally to sell weed. Her parents were not pleased, but Terri, though a nondrug-using "nerd," kept seeing this young man. Some of Terri's friends heard about her boyfriend's extracurricular activities and asked to be put in touch with him so they could buy a little weed for themselves. Terri made the introductions.

A week later, those classmates were caught smoking in school. They named both the boyfriend and Terri as the suppliers, which resulted in swift action: Terri was labeled a drug dealer. The Chicago public school's policy of "zero tolerance" stated that drug dealers were to be expelled from all public schools, meaning that Terri would not graduate high school and for that reason could not go on to college. A date was set for a public hearing to confirm her expulsion. It was the beginning of the end of her bright future.

Panicked, her family asked me to write a letter in support of Terri and to attend the expulsion hearing. I agreed. When the day came, I sat outside the hearing room with what really did seem to be an entire "village" of Terri supporters—teachers, the school principal, her parents, her pastor—all ready to serve as character witnesses.

I also saw twenty or so other students from the same neighborhood, all male and brown-skinned, waiting for their own expulsion hearings. I saw not one teacher, principal, pastor, or even parent there to support these young men. They waited alone, with no advocates or even friends to walk with them through this devastating, life-altering process.

Some people would say this is how the system ought to work. Terri might be one of the "good ones" who did not really deserve to be punished, but those boys with connections to drugs were getting what they deserved. That is a common way of seeing our failings, but it is not what I read in the Gospel of Matthew.

That book of the Bible starts strangely, and many people skip it, so perhaps you have not noticed what it says. It begins with a list of the male ancestors in the line that led to Jesus, a long list of fathers: "Abijah the father of Asa, Asa the father of Jehoshaphat, Jehoshaphat the father of . . ." That sort of thing. Forty-two generations down through the centuries, a whole lot of names, some familiar but some pretty much unknown even to scholars. Why start off with a long list of names including some mostly forgotten? Was there no schoolteacher in Matthew's time to tell him that introductions are the place to put your main idea? Did he forget to have a main idea? Or have we missed it?

Maybe the list of ancestors is meant to show off Jesus' good family. It links the founding Hebrew patriarchs Abraham, Isaac, and Jacob to the Hebrews' greatest king, David, and from David in turn to Jesus, like a line of spiritual royalty. That was a common way of portraying the powerful in the ancient world, where rulers, like many rulers today, were obsessed with position, wealth, and military might. Julius Caesar's family, for example, claimed to trace its ancestry back to Iulus, son of the Trojan prince Aeneas, son of the goddess Venus. Caesar's father, also called Gaius Julius Caesar, was the governor of the Roman province in Asia; his aunt was married to one of the most powerful men in Rome, Gaius Marius. And so on—everything about that royal family sounded perfectly powerful and accomplished, to promote a myth that the person at the end of this family tree comes from a blemish-free family. No flaws here! Ordinary people like you and me could never be like royalty, so very strong and rich and noble and perfect. Our place was to be their servants.

The lineage of Jesus, though, down through those forty-two

generations, does not offer a myth of power and perfection. His line starts with the Hebrew patriarchs, it is true, but the patriarch Jacob is described in the Bible as a cheat and a con man who conspired with his mother to rob his own brother of his birthright. Among the women listed in the Book of Luke as maternal ancestors of Jesus is Rahab, an alleged prostitute. All along the family line that leads to Jesus we find people who have committed murder, rape, and adultery. There is promiscuity and violence. Those of Jesus' forebears who are not seriously flawed are often simply anonymous, described as good but with no connections to military power, wealth, or aristocratic status. It can all seem a little strange. Here is Jesus, whom we might call the greatest spiritual superhero in Christian teachings, and *these* are his people? The Roman emperors would never have allowed their names to be mentioned alongside such flawed and ordinary folk.

Of course, Roman rulers had some serious human flaws too. Emperor Tiberius, who ruled Rome at the time of Jesus and sounded so perfect on paper, only became emperor after he divorced his first wife, Vipsania, the love of his life, to marry Julia, a widow at the very height of the Roman aristocracy. The new couple hated each other, and Julia would carry on with other men at night in the Forum, humiliating Tiberius with her public infidelities. Finally, according to the historian Tacitus, the emperor became so unhappy with Julia and with himself for betraying Vipsania that he left Rome to live far away on the island of Rhodes. The emperor of Rome quit his empire to live in the country. This was a family with its share of problems, but we only learn about their flaws in the history books. In the official account that established Tiberius's reputation, they sound perfect.

The writer of the Gospel of Matthew made a different choice, including flawed and simply ordinary people in the official family tree of the Messiah. That family tree offers a complex portrait of spiritual heroes who, despite their accomplishments and connection to divinity, remain imperfect, like any of us. And it suggests that even the most ordinary, flawed beings could be capable of the greatest spiritual achievements. God does not pick out a few perfect humans to be above the rest. God does extraordinary things through ordinary people. For that reason, the stories suggest, we should be very, very careful about discarding anyone based on their flaws.

To say that another way, we all need grace. In my church, on Ash Wednesday, we are reminded by the cross of ash drawn on our foreheads that while we have sacred potential, we are all fragile and imperfect. We recall the words of Ecclesiastes 3:20: "From dust you came, to dust you shall return." Dust is an imperfect building material. When a business is under construction, sometimes the construction crew posts signs that say PARDON OUR DUST to show that they are in the messy process of developing, working, breaking, and rebuilding. Every one of us could wear one of those signs.

When we fall short, as we all will, and we discover we cannot be perfect exemplars of anything that is supposed to make us worthy, then we either seek pardon, or we find ways to distract people from our dusty humanity. So much of our arrogance, pride, machismo, and discomfort with those unlike us is just distraction—a way to keep others from seeing our dust. We soothe our insecurities by making others feel insecure, we push others to the bottom so we can feel for a little while that we are on top.

Or we can ask for, and receive, pardon. We can say, in effect, "It's true, I'm dusty. Please pardon my dust." This is such a simple theological idea. God deeply loves us and will blot out our transgressions. We will be held to account for our actions, but there is also the possibility of grace, of forgiveness beyond what we deserve. Our tradition offers that hope of forgiveness, that second chance that none of us deserve but may still receive.

Tragically, there is another tradition in this country, a tradition at war with the sacred possibility of grace, a tradition in which some are not offered pardon but are instead exploited for the benefit of others who believe they are set above. In this country, that grim countertradition began with slavery. Some of God's children were singled out to be used like animals, their humanity and their souls denied.

Although slavery came to an end with the Thirteenth Amendment to the Constitution, that amendment included a loophole. It reads: "Neither slavery nor involuntary servitude, *except as a punishment for crime whereof the party shall have been duly convicted*, shall exist within the United States, or any place subject to their jurisdiction." This exception for enslaving convicts permitted the creation of Jim Crow laws in nine southern states, which criminalized actions as basic as jaywalking, vagrancy, and gathering in small groups. By enforcing these new laws, it was easy to fill the prisons of the South with Black, brown, and poor men, and to use their petty rule breaking—jaywalking, gathering in groups of more than two, as I have said—to justify working them as slaves. Their forced labor during their prison terms replaced the forced labor lost to southern landowners at the time of emancipation. In this countertradition, punishment was not a step in the rehabilitation of the lawbreaker but an economic benefit to be maximized by the punishers. Grace and restoration were utterly off the table. This denial of a basic tenet of our Judeo-Christian tradition became a fix for the southern economy.

After the freedom movement of the 1960s, as Michelle Alexander showed in *The New Jim Crow: Mass Incarceration in the Age of Colorblindness*, many of those Jim Crow laws were revoked, but a new system took its place. The war on drugs made the penalties for possessing the inexpensive cocaine of the inner cities, known as crack, one hundred times greater than the penalty for possessing the same amount of cocaine used in the wealthier, whiter suburbs. America's prisons filled again with poor, Black, and brown men. Soon America was incarcerating a greater percentage of our citizens than any country in the world.

The effects of this unchristian countertradition, supported by a contingent of white evangelicals, are still being felt in different ways in almost every institution of American life, including education. The "zero tolerance" policy that landed my church member Terri and her twenty brothers in line for expulsion hearings was part of the "tough on crime" rhetoric that has been used to fill the prisons since Reconstruction. Those flawed, ordinary young men waiting alone were like those flawed fathers in the ancestral line of Jesus. Yes, they had made mistakes. Yes, they had to be held responsible. But was there not a better solution than to leave their chances for a decent future in the overworked, distracted hands of bureaucrats tasked with nothing but punishment?

Our young lady sat down in the hearing room and poignantly spun her tale, telling the committee how she had become smitten with this older guy and his bad-boy image. We all testified about her exemplary character and her bright future, and the committee voted to rescind Terri's expulsion. The committee said that they were swayed not by the argument that she had done nothing wrong but by the overwhelming support from her family and her church. Expelling her, they found, would be a loss to her school and her—our—larger community. They decided that Terri would have to serve a suspension and perform public service, but she would be allowed to return to school, and in turn, she could graduate and go on to college. She was still held accountable for what she had done, but her future was restored. As I write this book, she is a college graduate living in Texas. She owns her own business, and her sister is planning to move in with her to start her own college education. Terri, we would probably say, was the sort of person who deserved pardon, a second chance.

As for the rest, the young men? It seemed they were the other sort, the undeserving, the exploitable. I knew what would come next. After quick hearings, not delayed by the words of anyone speaking up for their positive qualities or the good they might do in the future, they would be removed from the Chicago school system. Deprived of any chance to get the diploma that might help them get a solid job, they would be left to spend their days hanging out on the streets, where the best money they could make, by far, was by dealing drugs. Dealing would probably land them back in prison, and on it would go. While Terri had received restorative justice—justice combined with loving care both for her and for her community—these young men would get only retribution. No caring, no love—only raw justice served cold and a future, for many, of crime, incarceration, and a marginal life as a second-class citizen.

Here is the point that the Gospel of Matthew helped me to see: Terri did not get her second chance according to the rules. Instead, as the committee made clear, she deserved punishment, but they gave her a second chance because of her potential and the good she could do for her community. It was an act of grace, given in appreciation of her human promise, the light inside her. Terri's community hoped that she could share her gifts for decades to come. They refused to see her torn down for her flaws and thrown away.

Could the same thing have been done for those young men who, like her, faced expulsion and a bleak future for a teenage mistake? I wish we could have found ways to hold them responsible yet still extend them grace—not because they were blameless but for the sake of ourselves and our city.

We can choose to offer grace by working to put the lingering past of the Jim Crow laws fully behind us. We can choose to honor other traditions. In the Babemba tribe of South Africa, when a person has done wrong, members of the tribe gather around the accused in a circle. They speak to the accused one by one, describing good acts from that person's life, small and large, in detail. The point is not to shame or punish but to remind the person of how much good they contain. When it ends, the accused is welcomed back into the tribe with a joyous celebration, reminded of the goodness within and the better life still to be built.

I thought of that Babemba ritual when I read Laura Paddison's reporting in *HuffPost* about a program organized by the nonprofit law firm Prison Law Office for American prison guards. Fourteen guards from SCI Chester, a medium-security prison in Chester, Pennsylvania, were sent to work and receive mentoring for two weeks at Norway's Ringerike Fengsel, a high-security prison forty miles outside the capital city, Oslo. Since 1998, the Norwegian prison system has operated on the philosophy that losing your freedom is plenty of punishment, and that the time a convict is in prison should be used not to make them miserable but to prepare them to be good neighbors when they return to their communities.

Although they are restricted by a twenty-three-foot-high concrete wall, prisoners are treated humanely in a setting that is much more like a college dorm than an American jail cell. Inmates are connected to the health services and educational opportunities that could help them make a new start when they are released. Inmates even receive assistance in finding jobs and housing. They are held responsible, but they are offered grace. In the words of one of the visiting American prison guards interviewed for the article:

> We [in the American prison system] feel we're serving our communities by keeping these dangerous individuals enclosed from society.

Here [in the Norwegian prisons], I think they feel like they're serving their community, serving their society, by taking those dangerous individuals and changing them for the better. . . . I'd never really looked at my job as an opportunity to change somebody's life.

Even in a high-security prison, there is still the choice of whether to pursue cold justice or restorative justice. Even there, we could offer people the chance to say, "Pardon my dust."

My father, Rev. Otis Moss Jr., tells a story about preaching in 1962 at the Southern Christian Leadership Council's national convention in Birmingham, Alabama. Dr. King stood up to introduce my father, but as Dr. King began to speak, a self-professed "Nazi" rushed the stage to assault him. SCLC members pulled the assailant off Dr. King and prepared to turn him over to the police, but Dr. King said, "No. Bring him to the back room!"

The so-called Nazi was terrified. Those large ebony men muscled him into the back room against his will, and once there, even more men gathered around. He could not get away.

Then they prayed over him.

"Y'all could have killed me!" he cried when they were finished. "I thought you were going to kill me! But you prayed for me."

He seemed stunned.

The men he had come to harm had not harmed him in return, though they may have felt he deserved it. Instead, they had forced him to recognize the humanity of his victims and to wrestle with the damage his own act could have caused. Their goal was not to tear him down but to employ a redemptive and public strategy. They used Sun Tzu and Jesus as their guiding lights. They still turned him over to the police, but they left him amazed by grace.

8

Dance in the Darkness

Face Your Fears with Love

The light shines in the darkness and the
darkness does not overcome it.

JOHN 1:5

It is better to light one candle than curse the darkness.

REVEREND WILLIAM L. WATKINSON

Someone was in my house. It was the middle of the night but there was a noise that sounded like someone doing—I didn't know what. My wife, Monica, heard it too. She rolled over beside me on the bed and said, "Why don't you go check that out?"

I hadn't been asleep anyway. My mind was racing. Some unstable people, stirred up by misrepresentations in the media, had lately been making threats against Trinity.

We're going to bomb your church.

This was in 2008, during the presidential campaign. I was a young, unknown, rookie pastor, taking over from a beloved icon and community father. Some political provocateurs in the media had gotten their hands on sermons by my predecessor, Dr. Jeremiah A. Wright Jr., and they were using material in those sermons against one of our church members, Senator Barack Obama, as he ran for president for the first time. They found very little, actually, in Reverend Wright's great body of work that would compromise Senator Obama. Despite their furious efforts to defame, all they could find was a few words taken out of context from a powerful message—that is, a sermon—given when Obama wasn't even present. But the challenge for us in dealing with the national media was that most people in the television news audience had no personal experience of the Black church. Almost anything shown onscreen could be connected to racialized myths and stereotypes that catered to white anxiety: "This is not your mother's church!" Sean Hannity even showed a video clip of me at the start his inflammatory television program to drum up white fear and anger. Apparently, our worship of God was some kind of danger to America.

All that media attention had attracted unstable people and their threats. We were receiving at least a hundred threats a week, some by phone call, some by handwritten letter. The irony of using the tools of enlightenment was not lost on me: a number-two pencil and classroom notebook paper to express ignorance and rage. Still, the threats kept coming.

We're going to kill you.

Such violent words lingered in my consciousness, strange fruit demanding to be picked. And let me tell you: When you're up in the night worrying about death threats, the last thing you want to hear is unusual noises in your home.

I heard them again. Like a good preacher, I reached for my rod and staff to comfort me. This "rod and staff" was made in Louisville, with the name SLUGGER on it. Gripping that baseball bat in both hands, I searched downstairs, room by room. My heart pounding, I checked that the doors and windows downstairs were all closed.

Everything seemed in its place. Maybe the sound was nothing?

In those days, I was constantly afraid that I wasn't doing enough to protect my parishioners and my family. The challenges seemed to come from every direction: personal, political, professional. My soul seethed with fear. My ancestors down in Georgia would have said, "This is where the haints feed, at the kitchen with fear, at the table next to sorrow." *Haints* is a southern, African American term for ghosts of the mind and spirit who live on blues and despair. Modern academics categorize these folktales as antebellum vocabulary for depression and anxiety, but whether you know haints or Carl Jung, you can imagine how the spirit can be singed and the body weakened when haints, not saints, march in upon the mind.

Before then, I had understood in an intellectual way that fear was not only a feeling but a weapon. In the Bible, we read about how the Romans used fear to intimidate and control the Jews when the Roman army occupied Palestine. Howard Thurman called fear "one of the persistent hounds of hell that dog the footsteps of the poor, the dispossessed and the disinherited." Now, though, I could feel what he meant. Fear was a hellhound. If we cannot learn to confront it, it can destroy anything we are trying to build.

After searching the house, I yearned to go back to bed but I knew sleep would elude me. I thought about a sermon that I was struggling to write. Lately, I had not been feeling all that qualified to write sermons or to reassure anyone, even myself. Dr. Martin Luther King Jr. had taught the importance of living a "complete life," in harmony with ourselves, our community, and God. Was I in harmony? Not that night, I wasn't. Not much that week and not a whole lot that year. All too often, I was an anxious, distracted man, alone in the dark with his baseball bat and his fears. My soundtrack then was the old-school, Fifth Ward Houston hip-hop group, Geto Boys: "Mind Playing Tricks on Me." Even during the day, I felt the darkness. Fear was wearing me out, physically and spiritually.

That noise again! Coming from upstairs, clearly now, in the direction of my little girl's room—the last thing a father wants to imagine. I climbed the stairs, clutching that baseball bat. My thoughts were focused on one thing only: self-defense, that raw, pragmatic form of justice. If some unstable person filled with hate had broken into our home to do us harm, I would knock him out before he got the chance.

I reached my daughter's bedroom and pushed open the door, straining to see in the dim light.

"Daddy!" Makayla cried.

My little girl was out of bed, twirling around the room, her pigtails spinning this way and that. She was making the noise I had heard. There I was, trying to face a serious threat to our family, and she was pulling me out of bed with this childish nonsense.

"Go to bed, Makayla. It's three in the morning."

"Daddy! I'm *dancing*!"

"I can see that!"

Sleep deprivation mixed with irritation forced an exhausted and sharp, "Baby, go to bed." She had scared me pretty bad. And because she had awoken her parents in the night and added to our troubles, I might have extended my ire by going into "Dad mode," a stern, disciplined, lower-voice register. I could have reminded her that we had plenty of reason to fear. I might even have scared her myself, spoiling her night's sleep as mine had been spoiled. But at that moment I heard another voice.

Listen to her. Look at your daughter.

She was dancing a strenuous, joyful routine, no doubt inspired by the ballet lessons she was taking. Her movements were so jubilant, her spirit so free of worry or fear that I couldn't even stay mad at my baby girl.

She's dancing. The darkness is all around her as it's all around you—but she's still dancing.

In that moment, I saw beyond the threat that had been in my mind. Instead of seeing Makayla as just another addition to the night's problems, I glimpsed her as a fellow traveler. We both walked a dark path. Six years old, she could not have explained all the adult details of racism and politics, and I hoped she was not aware of all the doubt and insecurity her father sometimes felt. But I knew she sensed the darkness. No one living in our house could have missed the pressure we were under. We had protesters outside our church, up to forty news trucks lined up on our street, reporters calling out questions as we tried to get in through the church door. Her father was distracted and discouraged. Her mother was worried. Her parents got testy. Had she been unaware of all that, she could have done her dancing in the daylight. Instead, like her frightened father, this six-year-old fellow traveler was awake in the night.

Even so, there was a difference. I was caught in a cycle of worry and anger. I was not just walking a dark path; I had let the darkness inside me. Evil always seeks to obscure the light, because once it has you living in darkness, that which should not be painful becomes so. Even the sounds of a beloved, joyful child can become part of the anxiety, the torment.

Unless we have better guidance, our eyes go to the shadows, and as we peer into darkness and worry what may jump out, the shadows can become all we see. The truth I had forgotten was that only a few people in this world harbored genuinely malevolent feelings toward me. Only a few wanted to do me harm, but because I focused more and more on the darkness, I felt as if I lived in a world where every shadow hid a threat.

What we forget, faithwise, in our fear—what I was forgetting that night in my daughter's room—is that even in the darkest night, when we see no light at all, the light is still there. The sun is still shining over Earth even when our side of Earth rotates away from it. The stars still shine above us, no matter where we are or how thick the clouds above our heads. What we need in the darkest nights is to keep walking along the path until we can glimpse the stars again. What we don't need is to panic and run blindly into the woods.

Makayla was just a child, but on this night, she had moved ahead of me on that path. By dancing in the dark, by doing one of the things she most loved, she was making her own light. When she asked to show me her dancing, she was not just showing me childish play. She was demonstrating that she had found a personal connection to things she loved, and that love gave her sustenance and courage. She could dance with joy, then sleep deeply and wake up in the morning refreshed. In that respect, she was doing better than her dad.

I watched her dancing in darkness until she came to a natural pause, and as I watched, my love for her washed away my fear. I scooped her up and carried her back to her bed. After I kissed her goodnight, I made my way back to bed to see if I could possibly catch a few winks before the sun came up. Some of her joy, some of the light in her, was still with me as I lay down. I let go of my worry, closed my eyes, and slept until morning.

When I arose, I rushed to my desk to make some notes. The enduring words of Psalm 30 struck me afresh: "Weeping may endure for a night, but joy comes in the morning..." The eleventh verse of the Scripture made me shout: "You have turned my mourning into dancing."

• • •

My six-year-old had given me a much-needed reminder. With my vigilance and my baseball bat, I'd stood ready to meet the threat, and that threat was real. My family and my congregation were at risk of harm to both our persons and to our vision of a country where our differences enrich us all. But even as I fought against the real injustices of violent, racialized threats, I myself had been infected by darkness. It is the job of every preacher to teach the congregation how to wrestle with the darkness. In my fear, I had forgotten.

As I worked on my message, I thought of the words of Dr. King in his sermon "A Knock at Midnight." He said: "The dawn will come. Disappointment, sorrow, and despair are born at midnight, but morning follows. 'Weeping may endure for a night,' says the Psalmist, 'but joy cometh in the morning.' This faith adjourns the assemblies of hopelessness and brings new light into the dark chambers of pessimism."

From the pulpit that Sunday, I told the congregation that Makayla offered a reminder of how to walk the path through our personal darkness. "Night comes in all of our lives, but night is temporary," I told them. "We must learn to dance in the darkness until morning." Even when we must fight, we must keep our connection to love.

This was no simple, feel-good message to focus on the positive. Nor was I saying that, when threatened, you need only bring love and understanding into your heart and every problem will be solved. That will not cut it. If you hear someone breaking into your home, you may *need* that rod and staff. But there is a difference between responding to fear and letting it think, feel, and act for you, like a demon possessing you. Life's challenges require us to fight, but if all we can see are threats and how to fight them, we lose ourselves. As they say in the Pentecostal church, we must always be alert to the enemy who seeks to steal what is rightfully ours: our joy, our way of life, our connection to the divine. That enemy does not attack with guns or political libels. It attacks from within, with fear.

That Sunday, I told the congregation that we must meet the threats in our lives. We must fight for justice, for our safety, and for the right to live in a world where we can thrive. But even in the darkness of midnight we can maintain a connection to the light. When we cannot survive in darkness by using visual tools of sight, we still have internal tools of memory to remind us of our terrain. Until dawn comes, we need more than the determination to fight for justice. We need love to keep us from getting lost in distraction, love to keep us from falling into despair, love to help us restore ourselves, get back into harmony with ourselves, so we can last through that dark night.

"Dance," I urged them. "Dance in the dark!"

The night I heard Makayla dancing, the threat was only in my mind, but another day, as the barrage of hostile, provocative media continued, our church received a very unwelcome visit. An infamous fundamentalist Christian group from Kansas, the Westboro Baptist Church, followers of Pastor Fred Phelps, drove their vans to the South Side of Chicago. They came to draw attention and publicity to their supposedly righteous cause: the idea that America is wallowing in depravity and doomed to damnation.

It was a Sunday morning, and they caught our church, both its leaders and members of its congregation including Senator Obama and his family, by surprise. Some of the Westboro people carried signs with outrageous claims about abortion and our church, while others shouted racist epithets through megaphones. Mothers and grandmothers had to move through this gauntlet of provocation and hate while trying to shield their little ones. Our spiritual home was under assault. I was horrified. Sometimes, the monsters you fear are real.

I was also furious, and I knew I wouldn't be the only one. On the South Side of Chicago, some citizens have not yet been won over to the nonviolent methods of Dr. King. I knew that some of our "cousins" from the community, if provoked, would use more aggressive styles of conflict resolution. This was just what the Westboro protesters wanted, to get our members on video committing acts of violence. No matter that the Westboro folks had attacked us, that we had justice on our side, or that I longed to put those so-called "Christians" in their place—they would be able to portray us in the media as violent, accessing racial stereotypes to undermine our community. That would stir up even more anger in our village and draw greater scrutiny and harassment. Things would only get worse.

It was up to me to stop this oncoming disaster, to find within myself my spiritual center and the strength to stare into the abyss and not be overcome. How? I had no idea. But I did have the Black Spiritual Tradition to draw upon. These frightening, provocative tactics were old and familiar ones, long used against African Americans, designed to reinforce a story that says we are naturally violent, that we are like animals—that is, not really human. This was one of the worst lies told to justify slavery.

Fear, provoked by insults, intimidation, and physical pain, has been used for centuries as a weapon against us. In recent years, these tactics have come back with a vengeance, now aimed at a much wider segment of the American people. It was in response to these kinds of brutal tactics that the Kingian tradition of nonviolence was created. It began to dawn on me that the same tradition could guide me to meet the threat of these Westboro Baptist people.

As they waved their hideous signs and screamed their hateful slogans, I might have been forgiven if my mind had turned away from creative acts of love, but I focused on the members of my community and how much good I wanted for them. As I did, the Holy Spirit dropped an imaginative flash of inspiration on me: a plan to turn "what man meant for evil into what God designed for good."

I ran back into the church and found the members of the choir who were still in the atrium, preparing for their customary processional into the sanctuary. I gathered them together and gazed upon the group, the seriousness of the situation surely etched over my face. I leaned toward them and began talking: *This is what I need for you to do. Muster up the kind of faith our ancestors had. We are going to march outside and surround the protesters, but we are not going to touch them. We are going to sing to the glory of God so loudly that our voices, the voices of love, are going to drown out the shouts of hate.*

The choir loved it. They could confront the frightening forces of bigotry and intolerance with song. They went out there, a hundred strong, and got right up in the faces of the Westboro people singing "This Little Light of Mine." Try to imagine a sixty-eight-year-old grandmother, all of five foot four, getting in the face of a menacing, rather stout six-three gentleman from Kansas, clapping and singing with all her power as the protester tries to gather his composure. That man was almost pushed into the street because the power of the song made him lose his balance.

Four elderly women surrounded the "megaphone man." He couldn't get a word out. They just kept singing and clapping. They were not literally dancing (well, maybe a few of them were!) but the choir had found their own way to dance in the dark. They were fighting hate and fear with a song of spiritual power. It was beautiful.

We created a wall of sound so strong that the congregants could file into the sanctuary without hearing the horrific chanting. In my sanctified imagination, I saw the loving sound waves of gospel music wrestling the sound waves of hate. Somewhere between the lawn and the sidewalk, the words of hate decided to change course and join a new choir. The words of hate were not destroyed by the sounds of joy; they were transformed in midair.

I instructed the deacons to ask the protesters to join us in prayer—a simple request, one group of believers to another. (One could argue that we do not practice the same faith nor serve the same God, since our spiritual foundation is rooted in the belief that all human beings have dignity, agency, and the capacity to offer beauty to a broken world, while they believe . . . well, back to the story.) As I expected, the Westboro group rejected the chance to join us in lifting up the name of Jesus. But that didn't stop us from praying for them. They had offered us hate, but we offered them grace. The deacons joined hands and began to surround the protesters with Pentecostal prayer—that is, prayer deep from one's soul, designed by the spirit to place even a nonbeliever in a space of reflection. The atmosphere changed. The protesters were overwhelmed by something they were not used to: the spirit of God's love. Looking half drunk, they climbed clumsily into their vans and drove away.

There was no violence between our two groups, no damning coverage in the media, and no escalation of tensions. We had won ourselves a measure of peace. Something we could not have achieved by force or by calling the police, something no one expected we could have done—something that many people would have described, frankly, as miraculous—we had done by holding to the song and the prayer and the community we loved.

To practice spiritual resistance in the face of fear, we must remain connected, even in times of fearful threat, to what we love, those activities and people that bring us joy and feed our souls. Holding close to what we love roots us together. It strengthens and focuses us for the battles ahead. While some people might imagine loving and fighting as opposites, they are the kinds of opposites that need each other.

As a pastor, I collect and help others to identify those expressions of the greatest love and joy, to help release those habitual responses and recover moral imagination. For me, personally, I know that when I feel pressured, discouraged, or troubled, whether by events right around me or political news that makes my head spin, there is something about music that puts me in a different space. Music reawakens my sense of love and joy, reigniting my moral imagination.

But what will make the difference for me is not necessarily what will work for anyone else. Not long ago, I was talking to a buddy of mine who was telling me his worries and his fears for the future. I remembered how much he loved basketball, and I told him, "Man, take some shots. They've got a gym in the church, and you've done all you can do for today, so go grab a ball. When it's just you trying to put the ball in the basket, everything else goes away. You can pick up the other stuff again a little later on."

I know a woman who has been unusually successful in business, though no one had ever expected anything like that for her when she was a girl. She thinks about her most difficult challenges during the long runs, usually five miles, that she takes in the morning. Some people think she's a fitness fanatic and some people think she's just extremely introverted, but she's always loved running, and it makes her feel powerful and alive. When she's running, she can have her boldest ideas, think through her approach to her most intimidating meetings, and believe that she can attain her highest goals. Running every morning before she goes to work is her way of facing her fears and dancing in the dark.

The love that frees us to dance in the dark may come as part of a lifelong interest or practice; it can also come in a flash. As I was writing this book, I was often lifted up by the ridiculous, beautiful artistry coming out of the protests against new federal policies that sought to turn us against one another. I remember when the first executive order banning travel from Muslim countries went into effect. On television, I saw scenes of protest at an airport. A man who was African American was holding up a sign that read DO NOT DEPORT MY MUSLIM BROTHER! And next to him, a man who was Arab American held a sign that read DO NOT SHOOT MY AFRICAN AMERICAN BROTHER! That made me smile. Their creativity and humor gave me a moment of dancing in darkness, because those men had reminded me that I love our whole human family, and that our family laughs together.

We must cultivate what we love like a garden. It helps to be like Makayla that night, realizing that, even alone in darkness, without musical accompaniment, without a teacher or an accompanying dance troupe, without even a light on, she could still dance her ballet. We must cultivate our loves in bad times and good times, because the darkness will return and, with it, the hellhound of fear.

Even the Westboro Baptist Church, the protest group we had turned away with prayer and song, came back. They applied for a permit to stage a protest. Someone in city government who respected our work called to let us know that Phelps and his followers would be setting up across the street from Trinity. That gave us time to organize.

We asked many of our men to come to church early and stand outside, two lines of Black men standing along the sidewalk, so that if you were walking into church across from the protesters, you would have men standing on either side, and you wouldn't have to see the misleading posters, replete with insults, that the Westboro contingent carried. But the funny, inspiring thing was how some of our seniors, especially the women, after they had made it past the protesters and safely into the church, chose to walk back outside again and take another turn around the block. They said, "I want to walk past those good-looking men again!"

The love our men had for what we call the Trinity "village" inspired them to stand guard for us, and the love some of our older members felt for our strong, handsome men turned a moment of hatred and intimidation into a kind of celebratory dance. And in that way, our well-cultivated village love helped us stand up to an assault of fear. We got our members safely through the open doors of the church once again.

Epilogue

America and Amazing Grace

White Rage and the Colors of Hope

> *I'm gonna lay my head on that*
> *lonesome railroad track*
> *but when I hear the whistle,*
> *Lord, I'm gonna pull it back.*
> RICHARD M. JONES, "Trouble in Mind"

> We do not have much time. The revolutionary spirit is
> already worldwide. If the anger of the peoples of the
> world at the injustice of things is to be channeled into a
> revolution of love and creativity, we must begin now to work,
> urgently, with all the peoples, to shape a new world.
> DR. MARTIN LUTHER KING JR., *The Trumpet of Conscience*

I began this book with the opening of a letter I had written to my son. I wrote the letter after we had sat together and watched a video posted to Facebook. Elijah and I were two of the two and a half million people who watched the video that day. A woman named Diamond Reynolds made this video on her phone after she, her four-year-old daughter, and her boyfriend, Philando Castile, were stopped by a po-lice officer in a suburb of St. Paul, Minnesota.

In her video, Reynolds explains that moments before she turned on the camera, their car had been stopped by a police officer. Castile, an African American who worked as a nutrition supervisor providing food at a high school, was asked to show his driver's license and reg-istration. He complied. He also told the officer that he was licensed to carry a gun, which was in the glove compartment with those docu-ments. His response to the police officer was accurate, law abiding, and respectful, but in the officer's imagination it was so frightening, coming from a Black man, that he shot Castile, repeatedly.

The video continues as Ms. Reynolds, a bystander at this shoot-ing, is ordered to get out of the car and kneel to be handcuffed. In the car, Castile moans in pain as he bleeds to death. From the backseat, the little girl watches.

Sitting with my own fifteen-year-old child, watching a grown man die—seeing that man's dreams fade before our eyes while his loved ones were humiliated and terrified—I couldn't help but think, *There but for the grace of God go I.* I knew my family could be cast in the remake of this movie. I felt the full horror of the ongoing, racial-ized present, and I knew again how fully the statements "It is in the past" or "That was history, why bring it up now?" fail to comprehend the ways the past still shapes our imaginations, and how the racial-ized imagination can still destroy us.

I do not mean to suggest that I learned anything new. Rather, I felt the full pain of the truth I had sensed even as a young boy, ever since the day my best friend Nick and I discovered that the sight of eight-year-olds on bicycles was so terrifying to the imaginations of white drivers (if the eight-year-olds had brown skin) that they locked their cars.

How did we get here? What in our shared American history can explain the racialized imagination, which brings so much distrust, fear, and violence to situations where they are not necessary and make no sense? History for a parent of African American descent is both elusive and sacred. Elusive because of the hindrances, intentional and unintentional, that keep my family from a basic natural right: the ability to freely explore and to know our past. My name, my origins, and my complex ethnicity are all hidden or obscured by myths, tales, legends, and lies that create a false history and support a larger political and social agenda.

But if my history is elusive, it is also sacred. The Gospel of John carries an ancient lesson highly relevant for our still new republic: "Then you will know the truth, and the truth will set you free." Truth-telling is directly connected to love and the practice of justice. Love— *agape* love, *ubuntu* love—demands truth. As a parent, I am called to be a truth-teller and to equip my children to be unafraid of truth. It was necessary for me to write that letter because the truth is that my family today is bound up in its history, and our history is bound up with the racialized imagination.

That history is described in *Africans in America*, the book based on the public television series. Starting in 1562, a small group of English merchants seeking to make a profit in the New World hired an ambitious English adventurer named John Hawkins. His ships flew no colors; this pirate sailed as a rogue upon the seas into western Africa and came to possess three hundred "negroes" from Sierra Leone. He sold his captured Africans in Hispaniola, the island that is now divided between Haiti and the Dominican Republic, where the European colonizers' wars, enslavement, and disease had killed so many of the natives that there were not enough left to work the sugar plantations. Hawkins's trade in human flesh began the English role in what would become the transatlantic slave trade.

The market forces that drove the slave trade demanded a justification, something to ease the consciences of nations beginning to profit off this new, global, human-trafficking scheme. The men and women taken from Africa to become slaves came from highly accomplished civilizations, marked by centuries of technological innovation, far-ranging trade, and sophisticated political treaties, but this truth was too uncomfortable. Europeans began telling the story of Africa with all that history erased to make room for a myth: that dark skin was a scourge, the marker of a race of intellectual toddlers who might possess great physical strength but had inferior brains—and therefore needed to be controlled by Europeans. To justify their profits, in other words, they imagined an unholy horror: They allowed themselves to pretend that a group of human beings, made like themselves in God's image, had been created to be slaves.

As yet, though, across the ocean in the colonies of North America, there were no slaves and no motive for a racialized reimagining of people from Africa. The first Africans arrived on our shores by chance. In August of 1619, a Dutch ship robbed a Spanish ship of sugar, rice, and slaves, then ran into bad weather and other difficulties. The Dutch pirates, struggling to maintain their vessel and close to starving, dropped anchor in Jamestown, offering to trade twenty Africans to the Virginia colonists in exchange for food and shelter. John Rolfe, an English settler and the husband of Pocahontas, wrote about the arrival of the Africans to the colony: "About the last of August came in a Dutch Man of warre that sold us twenty Negars." A group of struggling pirates, desperate to live, had accidentally brought the slave trade to North America.

Among the historical records of Jamestown are two names: "Antonio, a negro," one of twenty sold from the Dutch man-of-war, who married "Mary, a negro woman" who arrived later aboard the vessel

Margaret and John. Antonio and Mary pledged vows to each other and before God, becoming the spiritual ancestors of all Africans in the New World, including—later, and in dramatic ways—my own family.

Until this point, the Virginia colony had no slaves, so it had no laws regarding slaves. Much of the work of growing tobacco was done by indentured servants shipped from England, drawn by the promise that after four to seven years of work, they would be set free and given a bushel of corn, a new suit, and a parcel of land. Everything about their new life was hard and dangerous, from their voyage across the ocean to the diseases of the New World to the back-breaking work in the fields. Of the first fifteen thousand who came to Jamestown this way after 1607, only two thousand survived. Housed in shacks, provided minimal food rations, and whipped for infractions of the rules, they were worked like slaves, but they were not slaves for life.

The twenty newly arrived Africans were seen not as members of a race removed from human dignity but as comparable in class to these indentured servants. The colony was full of servants and landowners, the indentured and the free, the commoners and the lords of the New World. Skilled labor and agricultural ingenuity were at a premium, and at least theoretically, anyone of any skin color had the opportunity to rise beyond their class boundaries. The word *white* was not a part of the New World vocabulary as a description of people. The racial slur "nigger" was not yet in use and would not be widespread for nearly two hundred years. Antonio and Mary would have been referred to as "African" or "Negro."

Records indicate that by 1650, Anthony (as he was now known) and Mary Johnson, former negro servants brought to America by an act of piracy and evil, owned two hundred and fifty acres of land stretching from the Pungoteague Creek on the eastern shore of

Virginia. These two stolen people of African descent were living a colonial American dream.

This African American couple was more fortunate than many of the Anglo indentured servants who often found that the landowners who had paid for their passage across the ocean would not honor their agreements to work only for a limited period of years. Even after the legally contracted period of service was up, these servants were not free to move to other employment or to negotiate new terms. Soon Africans and indentured Anglos began to recognize a common opponent in these unjust landowners. They began to fight together for self-determination.

Recognizing the threat, some landowners began trying to break the growing alliance between Africans and indentured Anglo servants. Instead of meeting the new demand among servants and former servants that landowners honor contracts and negotiate wages, they offered common laborers a new status as quasi-lords, well below landowners but now placed above Africans. Beginning in 1639, laws were put on the books to create American slavery. Under the new definition, the status of slave, which was different from and below that of servant, would be based not on the work performed but on the worker's race and country of origin: only non-Europeans would be slaves for life. As legal rights were stripped from non-Europeans, servants discovered privileges that had been reserved for them. As of a 1663 law in Virginia, a non-European's child was legally a slave, the property of the mother's owner. A European servant's child was still born free. Such privileges made the European servants symbolically part of the landowner class even though they did not share in the landowners' wealth or power.

This was the beginning of "whiteness," which had not existed before—until then, paler colonists had identified themselves as

Anglo or Irish, French or German, or one of many other ethnicities. These groups held various prejudices about one another as well as about Africans and the Indigenous peoples in the area, but they did not think of themselves as "white." In this way, these attitudes used to justify slavery, as David R. Roediger points out, created the first identity politics in America—white-identity politics. America entered into a new social contract, what philosopher Charles Mills calls the *racial contract*, which legalized the denial of legal protection to non-Europeans and furthermore denied recognition of those people as God's children, each created equal. It was, by design, an assault on both justice and love.

The thriving Johnson family eventually established a farm on three hundred acres of land called Tonies Vineyard. By the spring of 1670, when Anthony lay down and closed his eyes for the last time, this man—stolen from his home in what is now Angola, yet endowed with a resilient spirit to thrive in a strange land—left a legacy of achievement and wealth for his wife and children. But again, after his death, there were Anglos who seized opportunities to exploit the racial contract. An all-white jury determined that Johnson's remaining land in Virginia must be seized by the state, "because he was a Negroe and by consequence an alien." The two hundred acres disputed because of an unethical claim were given to John Rowles. The fifty acres that Anthony had given to his son Richard were given to a wealthy Anglo neighbor by the name of George Parker, even though Anthony's son Richard, a free Black man, lived on the property.

Had the Johnson family not been deprived of the land that was legally theirs, today they would be one of the wealthiest families in Maryland. But without a voice in government, allies on the ground, or institutions to lobby on their behalf, they fell victim to what became a familiar story: suspicion of Black achievement and the misuse of the legal system to allow wealth created by Black labor to be plundered by so-called white people.

We could say that this is distant history, a world away from my son Elijah and his family, except that, nearly three hundred years after Anthony and Mary Johnson lost their family legacy to the new racial contract, my own cousins in Georgia suffered a tragically similar fate. I know the following details thanks to the researchers Tara Dunn and Ariel Goeun Kong of the Civil Rights and Restorative Justice Clinic at the Northeastern University School of Law. They researched the historical record to reconstruct the life of my cousin Henry "Peg" Gilbert, a farmer and a deacon of the Union Springs Baptist Church.

Peg was on his way home after Sunday service on May 4, 1947, when he and others in the congregation heard a gunshot that was the result of an argument. A Black man, Gus Davidson, twenty-eight years old, had come home from Pittsburgh to visit his family. He had an accident when his car collided with a calf belonging to Olin Sands, a white man. Sands heard the crash and got out of bed to confront Davidson. Sands would say that Davidson pulled a gun on him. Davidson would say Sands came at him with a gun and he had fired in self-defense.

The chief of the Harris County police, unable to locate Davidson, arrested all the young man's family members: his father, mother, brothers, and teenage sisters. The family was jailed for weeks and beaten to encourage confession, apparently on the theory that the denial of justice to an entire Black family was a reasonable price for information leading to justice for one white man. But the jailed family provided the police with no useful information.

The police separately received a tip that Davidson had been seen on my cousin's property on the night of the argument, and so my cousin Peg was also arrested on suspicion of having possibly aided

Davidson. While in custody, Peg's brother-in-law attempted to visit him, but the two men were not permitted to meet. Peg, however, was able to yell to his brother-in-law as he saw him leaving the building. He said that he did not expect to get out of jail alive.

A few days later, still in jail, Peg was shot by the police in what they described as an act of self-defense. The coroner later found that his skull had been shattered and one of his legs was broken. He had suffered five gunshot wounds. His wife, Mae Henry, told a journalist that when she kissed her husband in his casket, it felt like "kissing a sackful of little pieces of bone."

With the head of the family dead, the family farm was now sold at auction—to a relative of the white neighbor, Olin Sands, and for less than its market value. Mae Henry, now a poor widow, moved to Detroit with one of her daughters, but the other three children were split up and sent to live with different relatives who could still afford to raise them.

This was life under the full force of the racial contract, hardly changed since the Johnsons had suffered a similar miscarriage of justice nearly three hundred years before. Prejudice and abuse of the legal system went hand in hand with the economic plunder of African American wealth for the benefit of some who considered themselves white. The racial contract was the legal and economic method, and the racialized imagination was the emotional alibi. It was that same racialized imagination that I discovered for myself, bicycling while Black near my childhood home in Ohio; the same racialized imagination that Philando Castile discovered driving while Black in Minnesota.

Can anyone doubt that it was necessary to warn my son?

Even those young people who receive the warnings and learn to see the racialized imagination for what it is still find some of their hopes and dreams deformed. I remember when Elijah and I watched the first episode of *Marvel's Luke Cage*, a television show based on the Black superhero who fights crime in Harlem with superhuman strength and unbreakable skin. Elijah said, "He's so cool! I wish I could be him."

At that moment, I seemed to feel the entire history of Africans in America bearing down on my child. However, I was less interested in my assumptions than I was in my child's own experience, so I asked, "Why is that? What's cool about him?"

"Bulletproof skin."

"Yeah?"

"You wouldn't have to worry if you got pulled over by police. Because you were bulletproof."

In my letter, I told Elijah:

I am sorry I must write this to you, but it is the duty of every Black father to share the stories of this battle with his son. It is unfair, but your capacity to handle the weight of this truth is evident through your spiritual maturity. And while I am bound by duty and love to share this truth, it is not the only truth you must know. What is often forgotten and deleted from your primary and secondary curriculum are these simple truths: You are a beautiful boy of color, a child of African descent, a magical creation of God.

There will be days that tempt your spirit to run to the room of despair and play the chords of cynicism, but do not shy away from the pain. Do not become a modern pessimist afraid to act, or one who believes that hope is nothing but a fairy tale. Dare to lean into the storm, son, and draw strength from the history you hold and the faith you profess. Not the faith others claim you hold, but the faith in which justice, protest, intellect, wonder, grace, righteous fury, and love do battle against the dragons fashioned by old men.

To some, it might have sounded as if I was "only" writing this letter to my child, "only" warning an African American youth about the ongoing dangers of the racialized imagination. But it is not only my children's bodies that are at risk, it is America's body politic. I wrote to my own son as a concerned father, but I could have been writing to any of God's children in America to show them the basis for meaningful hope.

So, please do not misunderstand me. I often hear Dr. King invoked today in the narrowest way, as a fighter for African Americans, a kind of tribal-identity politician. I also hear him cast as a kind of cheerleader, congratulating America for no longer judging people by the color of their skin. However, Dr. King only looked forward to the day when that would be true. He was articulating a dream for the future. In his life, he was always working against the racial contract because of the harm it does to this democratic experiment, the Black psyche, and the American soul.

As early as 1958, he observed that "poor whites are exploited just as much as the Negro." And after the successes of the 1960s in fighting Jim Crow laws and establishing a meaningful right to vote, he turned to a new phase of the movement, broadening the southern fight against racial humiliation into a national, nonviolent war for economic fairness. "The inseparable twin of racial injustice," he wrote, "is economic injustice."

In 1968, he launched the Poor People's Campaign to bring justice and opportunity to impoverished people of all backgrounds, from Indigenous peoples to Appalachian whites. He advocated for an alliance between the civil rights movement and the labor movement. Were he alive today, Dr. King would probably get accused of being a "socialist" or a "communist." These words are often used to attack those who stand up against injustice. So it is worth noting that Dr.

King had read deeply in the political philosophy of both capitalism and communism, and he had criticisms of both. "Communism forgets that life is individual," he wrote. "Capitalism forgets that life is social, and the kingdom of brotherhood is found neither in the thesis of communism nor the antithesis of capitalism but in a higher synthesis." His goal was not to elevate capitalism or to destroy communism, but to reunite ordinary Americans according to their shared interests, overcoming the division imposed by the racial contract ever since workers from European families were turned against workers from non-European families in Anthony Johnson's day. This second phase of the freedom movement was Dr. King's main project at the time of his assassination.

I began this book by observing that at this midnight hour, the country is coming apart, splitting in two in a kind of cultural civil war. We are still being divided by the racial contract, and the justification for this division is still the racialized imagination. The fears of those working people who have lost or could lose a degree of their accustomed status and success have been turned by unscrupulous leaders into a rage against all who look different, talk different, live different.

In this time of the systematic attempt to dismantle Dr. King's tradition of love linked to justice, with all it has accomplished, too many conservatives and liberals alike have fallen into parallel mistakes. On the left, too often we acknowledge the blues but leave out the gospel, the promise of the better world we seek to create. So the blues leads only to despair, an angry nihilism that, as the conservative columnist David Brooks has written, takes a negative view of American history and its achievements, seeing only "tales of genocide, slavery, oppression and segregation."

On the right, too often we deny the blues of this national midnight. We respond to any news of injustice by attacking the messengers, calling them unpatriotic. We attack the message by calling it "fake news." We denigrate the experts who have the knowledge and the artists who have the wisdom to show us how we live and how we fall short.

These reactions on the right and left may sound quite different, like opposites, but they are all ways in which Americans run from our national blues. Denial and despair are both ways to avoid wrestling with the spiritual challenges of our times. The alternative is neither to wallow in our blues nor to deny them, but to sing them. Of course, I do not necessarily mean singing musical notes into a mic. I am speaking of the diverse spiritual disciplines for nurturing your authentic voice to share your full story, pain and shame included.

This goes much further than singing along to release some feelings. The author Ralph Ellison defined the blues this way: "an impulse to keep the painful details and episodes alive in one's aching consciousness . . . expressed lyrically." Singing your blues means giving that ache in your consciousness, your blue notes, a form and a lyricism that can describe the precise demon that haunts you, until you both feel its harm and recognize where it comes from.

When you recognize those demons, as we have been trying to do in this book, we can go after them, in our hearts and in our body politic. And if we want a model of how that sort of politics would work, we need look no further than one of America's most unique and brilliant uses of the blue notes: jazz music. Jazz grew out of traditional blues music amid the extraordinary social forces merging in New Orleans, bringing together free Haitians, Africans, Native Americans, French, Spanish, and German, Italian, Irish, and Jewish immigrants into a gumbo culture born from the womb of the antebellum South. This white-supremacist nightmare gave rise to music that has African connections but is not purely African. It has European elements, but in no way could you call it European. It could only have been born in America, in the mixture of tragedy and triumph that defines the New Orleans experience.

One of jazz's unique elements is the musicians' ability to express individuality within a tightly disciplined group. Jazz takes instruments that traditionally did not play together and throws them all into the mix. The saxophone was devised for the marching band. The piano was traditionally used in European classical music, to be played in that modality. The bass was designed to be played with a bow, not plucked with the fingers. The trap drum set was intended to be played in a specific structured time, not freed up to play a variety of rhythms, syncopations, and colorations. Jazz composition dares to bring together these diverse instruments, cultural histories, and musical perspectives to play together, sharing the same melody, creating something out of our varied and sometimes ugly histories that is unquestionably beautiful. This is the hope of American democracy: individuals striving on their own to become more perfect, to create more beauty out of their own traditions, yet remaining true to the national group.

Where jazz ascends to majesty is in the improvisation. Every instrument has the right to its solo; no one tries to silence the others. That doesn't mean that jazz musicians exist in some peaceful utopia. They may not always like each other. They don't always get along. They are competitive sometimes to the point of aggression and prejudiced in all the usual human ways: The world of jazz musicians is a world that includes racism, sexism, homophobia, microaggressions, and plain, ordinary, old-fashioned aggressions. But they play together anyway. Whoever they are, they have in common a love for the music and a gratitude for their gifts. Every instrument is welcome. The piano doesn't say to the saxophone, *No, you need to sound like me.* The saxophone does not try to dictate to the bass—it just says, *Go ahead, do your thing.* Each has the right to solo, yet they are playing essentially the same themes.

Jazz, and all the many musical forms it has influenced, models a collective combination of love and the struggle for justice, because each instrument is saying to the other: *You have value, we all have value, and none of us is greater than the other.* This translates into: *We recognize your humanity. You may not sound like me, yet we are working together on the same themes.* In jazz politics, we define ourselves not by superiority to some denigrated other, but by how we use the gifts we were given to contribute to the community we share. In jazz, it is self-evident that all are created equal. In jazz, you can hear the sound of what Dr. King called the beloved community.

America lately has been fighting out its conflicting ideas of democracy in a very different form, through bullying words, impaired policy, civic discord, and intolerance. But America's uniquely original art form, jazz, was teaching America how to conduct a democracy before America even understood what democracy was all about. If we had a jazz version of democracy in our politics, where each of us could play all our notes, even the blue notes, and contribute them to the music of the whole, then dialogue and honest debate would be the norm rather than demonization and incivility. But in our stringent, ideological society, you must adhere to your side's doctrine—or else. Today, we seem not to believe in soloing or improvisation. We do not allow our politicians to hear blue notes and, in response, to grow and evolve. We want them to be consistent, which itself is a fallacy. When I listen to music, I don't want a musician who plays the same solo he learned back in high school. And when I hear a politician speak about an issue that pains and divides the country, I do not want a leader who holds the same position he's held since eleventh-grade social studies. I dream of a political class with the courage to stop shouting, and instead to hear and respond to the blue notes, to respond prophetically to the many sources of our grief, and to create a new song of a Just Love—Justice-centered love.

I must emphasize again that the kind of politics I dream of does not require us all to become friends or to hold hands. I am not waiting for a utopia—that is just another version of sentimental love. The politics I dream of can succeed if enough of us stand up for a Just Love, even though it will never be all of us. It will be enough. In my tradition, we say that even what man intends for evil, God can turn for good.

Perhaps my favorite example is the hymn "Amazing Grace." One of the best-known songs in the world, its beautiful words were composed by a former slaver. As a young man, John Newton, according to the Library of Congress, was dishonorably discharged from the Royal Navy on the open ocean and traded by his captain to a slaving ship. In his career as a peddler of Black flesh, Newton became known for his lack of religious faith and his hostility to the faith of his fellow sailors. Then in a terrible storm, with the crew and its human cargo all in fear for their lives, a wave swept another man overboard to his death. Newton felt that he himself survived only by the grace of God.

Over the next few decades, Newton gave up his life as a slave trader and became more religious. He was ordained as a minister in 1764, and in 1772 he wrote a poem called "Amazing Grace," based in part on his memory of the terrible storm from which he was saved. A few years later, he published an essay in opposition to slavery, adding his voice to the growing majority who stood up to say that it was inhumane. In 1807, Britain abolished the slave trade.

How did the English poem "Amazing Grace" come to America and then transform into one of our most beloved songs, known around the world? There are differing accounts. One explanation is that the poem was put to the tune of an existing hymn. Another, passed from mouth to ear by the stolen children of God whom Newton was transporting, says that while the storm raged, the slaves confined below the deck were humming, an extraordinarily beautiful sound that rose from the hull of the ship. The sound was so extraordinary, the story goes, that it reached the edge of heaven and an angel tapped God on the shoulder to say, "Creator, you must hear your children sing." And God bent over the banister of heaven and touched his finger to his lips, saying, "Hush, I want to hear my children." The storm suddenly ceased, and slaver and human cargo both were saved, and the seeds of faith and of a great hymn were planted in the soul of a religion-hating slave trader.

Ethnomusicologist and musician Wintley Phipps, who studies the musical structure of hymns, points out that the music of "Amazing Grace," which is uncredited, is structured on the African pentatonic scale, familiar to North Americans and Europeans as the black keys on the piano. Hymns were generally not structured on that scale, but the African-inspired religious music we call spirituals were. Phipps has deduced that the hymn "Amazing Grace" is a European text written to an African melody. You cannot play it without the black keys. If you tried, it would still be grace, but it would not be amazing.

That poem by the formerly anti-religious slaver became one of the most important hymns in the world, a global anthem of love and justice. It was a global, interracial collaboration unplanned by human composers. Like a great jazz improvisation, it took its contradictory parts and made something miraculous.

This is the heart of the Kingian tradition, but of course, the man himself is many years gone. People often ask me where we will find the next Martin Luther King Jr. I tell them we do not need one. We need hundreds of Kings. We need thousands. We need Kings and queens,

Frederick Douglasses, Robert Smallses, Anne Julia Coopers, Ida B. Wellses, W. E. B. Du Boises, Malcolm Xes, Fred Hamptons, Ella Bakers, Fannie Lou Hamers, Toni Morrisons, bell hookses, princes and princesses, warriors and priestesses, local superheroes, and freedom fighters by the millions—all working to build what Dr. King called a complete life, all refusing rage and choosing instead the colors of hope, all fighting like hell for justice and for love.

It was in this spirit that I ended my letter to my son and to all of us:

Never let your anger become unchecked rage, scratching at the lining of your heart. I tell you often, you are loved and designed with purpose and immeasurable potential. You carry a lineage of women who refused to bow and men who dared to live. Never forget who you are and the legacy you hold. The world we live in will attempt to steal your essence and drain away every ounce of your beautiful life from your soul. Never allow the external noise to disrupt your inner life. The practice of silence, meditation, prayer, reflection, community gathering, and healthy grieving will serve to strengthen you on this journey.

You and your generation are the gifts God has sent to victims of an old story. You are the prey of this nation's dying wolves who want yesterday always to be tomorrow, yet you are the solution to this nation's deepest problems. You are their fear, yet you are our joy.

I shall always be with you, though it is my prayer that my physical body shall precede you in death. This is the silent request of all parents, especially those of us who still wait to sip fully from the cup of democracy. It is my prayer that I will leave you the best fuel for this struggle for justice—my love. I love you and shall always fight for you and with you. Be well and be strong. Better days are ahead if you choose to fight with your head and heart.

Acknowledgments

Books are collaborative efforts rendered through the creative support, patience, and partnership of loving people.

Monica, my partner, wife, friend, and adviser for over twenty-eight years of marriage, pushed me to create a project that spoke to the internal and external spiritual needs of our community. If there ever was a "ride or die" person, you embody this ideal. I thank you for being my blessing.

Elijah, thank you for hours of conversation about music, movies, sports, politics, and theology—and for recommending I watch *Atlanta* and *Peaky Blinders*.

Makayla, your insight, artistic eye, humor, and example as a little girl dancing in the darkness set the stage for this book.

Mom and Dad, you laid the foundation with a living example of the power of Black spirituality. So much in these pages is an extension of your loving witness and wisdom.

My big brother, Kevin, your playful humor, loyalty to family, commitment to "the grind," and love of music made an impact on me before I could articulate that influence.

Daphne, my big sister who is now an ancestor, it was you who introduced me to jazz, to Toni Morrison, Zora Neale Hurston, and the poetry of Nikki Giovanni and Maya Angelou. One day I shall be able to write like you.

Momma Brown (a.k.a. Deborah, Nonni, mother-in-love—not law—the tiny tornado), thank you for being a sparkling container of joy for our family and a volunteer copy editor for this book.

Melody Morgan, I thank you for being the masterful magician who organized my insane calendar to create the space to sequester myself and write.

Gregory Lichtenberg, it has been a joy working with you. Your structural suggestions, editorial knowledge, skillful understanding of literary flow, and persistence were invaluable to moving this project from conception to reality.

Jennifer Gates and Todd Shuster, your professionalism, compassion, and counsel blessed this book. I look forward to many more projects in the future.

Mindy Marqués and Hana Park, our literary shepherds for this project. Thank you for protecting this book with your "rod and staff" and guiding it through the valley. My gratitude goes as well to Mark LaFlaur, the production editor, and Bob Castillo, the copy editor. And a shout-out and thank you to Dawn Davis, the editor who originally procured this project for Simon & Schuster.

Latanda Graves, Deacon Donna Hammond, and Deacon Lawrence "West Side" Myles, I thank you all for allowing me to share your beautiful stories of resilience and faith.

Trinity United Church of Christ, "the greatest church this side of the Jordan," I thank you all for allowing me the space to teach and preach these ideas. I do not believe there is a pastor as blessed as I am to serve a church unashamed about being Black and unapologetic about serving a loving Christ.

Mercer University's McAfee School of Theology, thank you for the opportunity to teach the ideas of democracy, jazz, cinema, comics, black spirituality, and preaching to such a wonderful group of students.

Dr. Michael Eric Dyson, I thank you for your friendship, mentorship, and hours of arguments about who is the true G.O.A.T. on the basketball court. Your foreword was a "Dysonian" masterwork.

Julian Gaines, watching you grow as an artist has been a blessing for our family. Thank you for offering a rendering of what *Dancing in the Dark* could mean on canvas.

And to anyone I forgot, in the words of our elders, "charge it to my head, not to my heart."

Notes

Chapter One

9 *"Public education for Black children in Daytona"*: Howard Thurman, *With Head and Heart: The Autobiography of Howard Thurman* (New York: Harcourt, 1979).

13 *"Fairy tales are more than true"*: attributed to G. K. Chesterton by Neil Gaiman in the epigraph of *Coraline* (New York: HarperCollins, 2002).

15 *"[Love] does not dishonor others"*: 1 Corinthians 13:5–7, New International Version (NIV).

17 *"I was hungry and you gave me nothing to eat"*: Matthew 25:42–43 (NIV).

Chapter Three

36 *versions of the "good" Samaritan story:* In early Christian times, Samaritans and Jews were all viewed as Jewish, and the term "good Samaritan" included an implied slur against Jews. Like the term "good Negro" in American history, it suggested that this particular Samaritan was one of the rare good ones. We use the term "good Samaritan" today while forgetting its origins.

Chapter Five

61 *"One day you finally knew"*: Mary Oliver, "The Journey," *New and Selected Poems, Volume One* (Boston: Beacon Press, 2005).

66   *"I am somebody"*: William Holmes Borders, "I Am Somebody," *The Pittsburgh Courier*, February 20, 1943, https://www.newspapers.com /clip/1206542/i-am-somebody-by-dr-william-holmes/.

Chapter Six

70   *"Through violence you may murder a murderer"*: Martin Luther King Jr., "Where Do We Go from Here?" *A Gift of Love: Sermons from "Strength to Love" and Other Preachings* (Boston: Beacon Press, 2012).

72   *record numbers of hate groups:* Heidi Beirich, "Rage Against Change: White Supremacy Flourishes Amid Fears of Immigration and the Nation's Shifting Demographics," *Intelligence Report* (Spring 2019, no. 166), p. 36.

74   *"Forgiveness does not mean ignoring what has been done"*: Martin Luther King Jr., "Loving Your Enemies," *A Gift of Love: Sermons from "Strength to Love" and Other Preachings* (Boston: Beacon Press, 2012).

74   *"Even if nonviolence isn't always the answer"*: Ta-Nehisi Coates, "Killing Dylann Roof," *The Atlantic* (May 26, 2016), https://www.theatlantic .com/politics/archive/2016/05/dylann-roof-death-penalty/484274/.

75   *"Envy not the oppressor"*: Proverbs 3:31. Translated by Otis Moss III.

75   *"The master's tools will never dismantle the master's house"*: Audre Lorde, "The Master's Tools Will Never Dismantle the Master's House," *Sister Outsider: Essays and Speeches* (Berkeley: Crossing Press, 1984), 110–114.

76   *"Darkness cannot put out darkness"*: Martin Luther King Jr., "Loving Your Enemies," *A Gift of Love: Sermons from "Strength to Love" and Other Preachings* (Boston: Beacon Press, 2012).

78   *"For You created my inmost being"*: Psalm 139:13–16 (NIV).

78   *"Neither death nor life"*: Romans 8:38–39 (NIV).

79   *"the evil act no longer remains as a barrier"*: Martin Luther King Jr., "Loving Your Enemies," *A Gift of Love: Sermons from "Strength to Love" and Other Preachings* (Boston: Beacon Press, 2012).

79   *the military strategist Sun Tzu advised:* Sun Tzu, *The Art of War* (New York: Basic, 1994).

80   *"The plant of freedom has grown only a bud"*: Martin Luther King Jr.,

"Where Do We Go from Here?" *A Gift of Love: Sermons from "Strength to Love" and Other Preachings* (Boston: Beacon Press, 2012).

Chapter Seven

86 *Jim Crow laws were revoked, but a new system took its place:* Michelle Alexander, *The New Jim Crow: Mass Incarceration in the Age of Colorblindness* (New York: The New Press, rev. ed. 2020).

87 *Soon America was incarcerating a greater percentage:* Mark P. Fancher, "Where Incarceration Isn't the Answer," *Yes!*, November 3, 2020, https://www.yesmagazine.org/issue/what-the-rest-of-the-world -knows/2020/11/03/where-incarceration-isnt-the-answer.

89 *"We [in the American prison system] feel we're serving our communities":* Laura Paddison, How Norway Is Teaching America to Make Its Prisons More Humane," *HuffPost*, August 22, 2019, https://www.huffpost.com/entry/norway-american-prison-system -reform_n_5d5ab979e4b0eb875f270db1.

Chapter Eight

93 *"one of the persistent hounds of hell":* Howard Thurman, *Jesus and the Disinherited* (Boston: Beacon Press, 1996).

Epilogue

107 *Starting in 1562, a small group of English merchants:* Charles Johnson and Patricia Smith, et al., *Africans in America* (San Diego: Harcourt Brace, 1998), 10ff.

111 *attitudes used to justify slavery . . . created the first identity politics:* David R. Roediger, *The Wages of Whiteness: Race and the Making of the American Working Class* (New York: Verso, 2017).

111 *America entered into a new social contract:* Charles W. Mills, *The Racial Contract: 25th Anniversary Edition* (Ithaca, N.Y.: Cornell University Press, 2022).

115 *"poor whites are exploited just as much as the Negro":* Martin Luther King Jr., *Stride Toward Freedom: The Montgomery Story* (Boston: Beacon Press, 2010).

115 *"the inseparable twin of racial injustice . . . is economic injustice":* Ibid.

116 *"Communism forgets that life is individual":* Martin Luther King Jr., "Where Do We Go from Here?" *A Gift of Love: Sermons from "Strength to Love" and Other Preachings* (Boston: Beacon Press, 2012).

117 *"an impulse to keep the painful details and episodes alive":* Ralph Ellison, *Living with Music: Jazz Writings* (New York: Modern Library, 2002).

120 *As a young man, John Newton:* Jonathan Aitken, *John Newton: From Disgrace to Amazing Grace* (Minneapolis: Crossway, 2013).

121 *the music of "Amazing Grace," which is uncredited:* Wintley Phipps, "History of Amazing Grace," https://www.youtube.com/watch?v=FPM biEkLK7E.

About the Author

The Rev. Dr. Otis Moss III is senior pastor of Trinity United Church of Christ in Chicago, Illinois. He is a preacher, poet, activist, author, community organizer, scholar, filmmaker, and the founder of The Unashamed Media Group. In October 2020, Dr. Moss created *Otis' Dream*, a short film about his grandfather's unsuccessful attempt to vote in 1946. The film has received numerous awards and acclaim across the country.

Dr. Moss was identified by the Baylor University George W. Truett Theological Seminary as "one of the twelve most effective preachers in the English language" in 2018. Along with his ministerial duties, he is also a Professor of Homiletics at Mercer University's McAfee School of Theology in Atlanta, Georgia. He is married to Monica Brown-Moss, and they are the grateful parents of the amazing team of MK (Makayla) and Elijah.